Cycling for Women

Savvy Advice from the Sport's Leading Women Writers

EDITED BY ED PAVELKA

Rodale Press, Inc.
Emmaus, Pennsylvania

Bicycling is a registered trademark of Rodale Press, Inc.

Printed in the United States of America on acid-free ∞, recycled paper ♻

Cover and Interior Designer: Susan P. Eugster

Photograph on page 28 courtesy of Terry Precision Cycling for Women
Photograph on pages 108–9 courtesy of Trek

"Handling Harassment" on page 12 reprinted with permission from *A Woman's
Guide to Cycling* by Susan Weaver, Ten Speed Press, Berkeley, California

Library of Congress Cataloging-in-Publication Data

Bicycling magazine's cycling for women : savvy advice from the sport's leading
   women writers / edited by Ed Pavelka.
      p.   cm.
   Includes index.
   ISBN 1–57954–169–0   paperback
   1. Cycling for women.   I. Pavelka, Ed.   II. Bicycling.
  III. Title: Cycling for women.
  GV1057.B53   1999
  796.6'082—dc21   99–39466

Distributed to the book trade by St. Martin's Press

2   4   6   8   10   9   7   5   3   1   paperback

Visit us on the Web at www.rodalesportsandfitness.com,
or call us toll-free at (800) 848-4735.

OUR PURPOSE

*We inspire and enable people to improve
their lives and the world around them.*

Notice

The information in this book is meant to supplement, not replace, proper road cycling and mountain biking training. Like any sport involving speed, equipment, balance, and environmental factors, cycling poses some inherent risk. The editors and publisher advise readers to take full responsibility for their safety and know their limits. Before practicing the skills described in this book, be sure that your equipment is well-maintained, and do not take risks beyond your level of experience, aptitude, training, and comfort.

Contents

Introduction vi

PART ONE

The Power of Cycling

1 A Note from Connie 3
2 Keeping Up with Him 4
3 Riding with Confidence .6
4 Street Savvy 9
5 After the Fall 14

PART TWO

Made for Women

6 Breaking the Bounds 19
7 Perfect Match 21
8 Do You Need a Women's Bike? 26
9 Have a Seat 30
10 Clothes with Wheel Appeal 35

PART THREE

Mechanical Matters

11 Fit for the Road 41
12 Fit for the Trails 44

13 You, the Bike Mechanic 48
14 It's Easy to Fix a Flat 50
15 Simple Bike Care Tips 55

PART FOUR

Body Talk

16 Cycling during Your Cycle 63
17 Riding while Pregnant 65
18 Make a Muscle 70
19 Love Your Butt 74
20 Now, about Your Diet 77
21 Key Questions Answered 85

PART FIVE

Opportunities

22 Women's School for Roadies 93
23 Playing Dirty 98
24 It's Never Too Late 101

Anatomy of a Bike 108
Glossary 111
Index 115
About the Authors 121

For the latest news, product information,
and training tips, visit our Web sites at
www.bicyclingmagazine.com and www.mountainbike.com
BICYCLING. **Mountain BIKE.**

Introduction

During my dozen years as executive editor of *Bicycling* magazine, we occasionally annoyed some female readers despite our best intentions. Why? Because we wrote articles specifically for women. And now, looking back, I really can't blame those who became upset.

Here's what happened. We knew that half of all adult bike riders are women, even though there's no disputing that cycling is a male-dominated sport. Women simply weren't as visible because not a high percentage of them raced, trained rigorously, or rode the long-distance events that defined *Bicycling*'s readership of "fast recreational cyclists." Okay, so how could the magazine welcome more women into the world of "serious" cycling? The answer seemed obvious: Create special sections and even entire issues just for women. Show them how to train, eat, ride with more skill, and graduate to challenging events. So that's what we did, and then were surprised that this seemed to bother about as many women as it pleased.

The backlash was usually expressed like this: "Don't make women seem like a separate group that needs special treatment. We're cyclists just like men." Had we made too much of the gender difference? After all, women and men are identical when it comes to almost every aspect of riding technique and training. On the other hand, there certainly are anatomical, physiological, and social differences. These are the real issues that set women cyclists apart.

Bicycling addressed them by instituting "Women's Cycling," a monthly column written by women, for women. While most of the magazine remained unisex and applied equally to all cyclists, this column explored subjects that women don't share with men. Included were discussions on female health issues, how women should respond to the sport's risks, and clothing and equipment designed specifically for the female body.

In this book, you'll find information on these topics plus other essential information. It's all geared to women who are relatively new to cycling and still learning the sport, helping smooth their way to many years of fun and fitness. For all of the unisex advice—expert information about how to train and ride more skillfully—we invite you to read *Bicycling*'s monthly issues and the other books in this series.

PART ONE

The Power of Cycling

1
A Note from Connie

Connie Carpenter is arguably the greatest woman cyclist in U.S. history. After scores of victories, she rode her final race in 1984—and what a farewell it was as she won the first-ever Olympic road race for women. Now married to ex-pro Davis Phinney, they are raising their family in Boulder, Colorado, and operating the Carpenter/Phinney Cycling Camps. Here, Connie tells us why she believes that cycling is a perfect sport for women.

One summer at our Carpenter/Phinney Women's Bike Camp, I saw that cycling can transform your life. On the first night, as we sat in a circle and talked about why we were at camp, one uncertain person said it was only because someone else had made her come. That someone, sitting across the circle, winced. We all laughed.

As the week progressed, this woman found that despite her initial fears, she could keep up, she could ride in a paceline, she did fit in. By the end of the week, it was clear that she had accomplished something long-lasting. The power of the cycling experience is just that simple. By meeting the challenge, by riding swiftly and strongly, by letting yourself be buoyed—not bullied—by a group, there is grace and power and joy. This spills over to everything you do, every day.

Cycling has allowed me to distinguish myself. It has enriched my life and empowered me. When I raced, I took riding for granted. But now, as the mother of two children and manager of my own small business, my rides often resemble a carefully planned escape: check weather, call babysitter, get dressed, turn on answering machine. Go!

My bicycle gives me an escape, my body supplies the power, the roads and trails provide the route. Every ride is a gift. A good ride fills me with hope, rekindles my childish sense of adventure, helps me conquer—or at least accept—fear, and lets me check the boundaries of my fitness. No ride is without challenge. Every ride is an adventure.

Meeting that challenge gives me the power and the sustenance not simply to endure but to enjoy, even savor, daily duties. What's more, almost every time I ride, I learn something new about myself, my environment, or the people I meet and ride with.

3

As a group, women who ride bikes are extraordinary. Why? Because cycling is a complicated sport, involving maintenance of the bike, the body, and the soul. Women have accomplished extraordinary and often unpublished feats on the bicycle. With due respect to every star racer, consider these two examples.

1. One woman who attended our camp had a pacemaker that limited her ability to extend herself and find her limits, yet she demonstrated enormous talent on her bicycle. After camp, she had a more turbo-charged pacemaker installed, partly because it let her ride harder. The lion in *The Wizard of Oz* was right—it takes heart to have courage. At age 40, this woman set the standard for being the most inspirational.

2. Thea Phinney is best known as the proud mother of my husband, Davis, a winner of two stages in the Tour de France. But Thea began to ride her own bike regularly. One summer, she set her sights on riding the notoriously difficult l'Alpe d'Huez during a trip to France with a bicycle tour group. Once she conquered the long, steep climb, she learned that at 71, she was the oldest woman on record to have done so.

Women who ride bikes are different. The challenges and accomplishments of every single day may not be recorded, but they will be remembered. Whether you use your bicycle for escape, as a means of increasing your fitness, or to become world class, the bicycle frees you. This is the gift of cycling. Take it. Enjoy it.

2

Keeping Up with Him

BY DEBRA BAUKNEY MOSS

It pains me greatly to admit I took up cycling to avoid housework. Every Sunday, after hours of tapping his lactic acid reserves with the guys, my husband, Hunter, would roll in, drop his sweaty clothes on the just-cleaned floor, trash the bathroom with a long shower, and destroy the kitchen making a breakfast big enough for 10 men. Then he would beg and barter for a leg massage and fall into a 2-hour nap on clean sheets. One day, I said to myself, "This stinks."

It occurred to me that if I started cycling, I could avoid Sunday dates with the laundry hamper. And wouldn't it be cool to eat like that? Was I the only misinformed cretin on the planet who fantasized about romantic sunset rides with a fanatic cyclist?

Knowing that I've nursed a pack-a-day habit since age 15, Hunter realized the shape my lungs weren't in and chuckled whenever I used the words "me" and "bike" together. When he could stand my pestering no longer, he leveled with me: "You'd never be able to keep up with us." When he saw my face go from hurt to furious, he caved. "Okay. Quit smoking and we'll buy you a bike." Lord have mercy on my tar deposits.

We lived on Saint Croix then. The Caribbean island hosts a triathlon known for a 700-foot vertical climb. The first time I clawed my way to the top of it my lungs felt like I'd inhaled butane and sucked a lit match. Hunter said, "Hey, you didn't vomit!" So much for romantic fantasy.

Many hills later, though no longer coughing up a lung, I still could not keep up with the guys. Sometimes, I just turned around and went home in disgrace. My husband would ride with me only when he was (a) nursing an injury, (b) needing a recovery spin, or (c) paying off a massage barter. I took whatever crumbs I could get.

I eventually got good ("for a woman"), only I had traded the boredom of ironing Hunter's shirts for the frustration of trying to keep his butt in view. He advised me to ride with women, but Saint Croix's roads are narrow, winding, and steep—too intimidating for all but the fearless. What few women rode were intrepid mavericks. Short of buying a Harley, I could not foresee how to feed my addiction for flying down long hills with the wind in my face. I came close to retiring.

It was the thought of returning to the Sunday cleaning routine that drove me to subterfuge—like the "tortoise-and-the-hare" ride. Hunter and I would agree on a route, then I would sneak out of the house ahead of him. When he discovered I'd left, he'd race to catch me. He got his power ride, and I pushed hard to lengthen the time till he reeled me in. Before long, sometimes he couldn't.

Together, we also instituted a short "loop-de-loop" course. Each time our paths would merge, we agreed he would not speed up and I would try to hang with him as long as my short little legs would hold out. Once I dropped, he'd speed up quietly on the next circuit and pinch me.

While these games hardly met the criteria of romance, they helped alleviate some of the frustration that was spoiling cycling for me, and it made us both better cyclists. Then one day, Hunter kept looking behind him and I was right on his wheel, mile after mile, with a huge grin on my face.

Over time, I think Hunter actually began to enjoy riding with his wife. Perhaps cycling together rekindled some of the fun he used to have before speed and pain became his objectives. My reward for refusing to give up was recapturing the freedom I'd felt as a 3-year-old, zooming down the sidewalk on my first bike. It also gave me back my health.

Now, if I could only get Hunter to iron my shirts.

3
Riding with Confidence

BY SARA J. HENRY

I remember the first time I discovered I could change a flat tire. My friend Ann was there, too, and she was just as much of a mechanical neophyte as me. We'd gone for a road ride on a beautiful day, but with just 5 miles remaining, disaster struck: a puncture.

Today it wouldn't faze me in the least, but back then, never having changed a tire, I thought it was a very big deal indeed. So big in fact, that Ann and I took the risk of leaving her alone, stranded by the side of the road, while I rode 3 miles to the bike shop in the hopes of getting my buddy Eric to drive out and help us. But he had gone on a lunch break, so back I rode to inform Ann that we had to change it ourselves.

We didn't set any speed records, but we did it. And the resulting feeling was euphoric. Confidence streamed through me with the realization that here was one thing I need never worry about again.

It's true that a woman is more likely to run into serious trouble on a bike than, say, walking across a mall parking lot, so it sure doesn't hurt to decrease the chances of trouble and prepare for it as much as possible. Consider the following precautions and learn what I did—that knowledge can empower you and increase your safety, skill, and confidence.

Steps to Prevention

Never let mechanical failure strand you. Buy or borrow a book on bike repair. Then practice the most common repairs. Mechanical skills will minimize the time you're vulnerable on the side of the road, and you won't have to hitch home or go door to door looking for a phone. Always carry some change, ID, a spare tube, a patch kit, tire levers, a pump, and one of those handy multitools with allen wrenches and screwdrivers. For basic mechanical tips, see part three of this book.

Circumvent trouble. When a car cuts you off or nearly hits you, stifle your urge to shout or gesture. You're putting yourself in danger when you anger someone at the controls of a big motorized machine. If you let it go, you'll forget all about the close call in a few minutes. But if you get into it with the driver, it'll be on your mind for days and will tarnish your enthusiasm for riding.

Wear looser clothing. Yes, we should be able to dress as we like, but some yahoos are still convinced that form-revealing clothing means you'll welcome their advances. If you're riding solo, looser jerseys or T-shirts and baggy shorts are advisable, says Dave Glowacz, an instructor in the Effective Cycling bicycling education program and author of *Urban Bikers' Tricks and Tips.* Glowacz also suggests hiding long hair in your helmet or under a jacket.

Ride a beater bike. If you ride for regular transportation, your worst fear may be a stolen or hijacked bike. The solution is simple. Don't use a bike that anyone would want to steal. Ride an old, scarred bike with heavy-duty wheels and tires that thwart punctures. To those who use them, such bikes are affectionately known as beaters. Or do as Glowacz suggests and "uglify" your bike by putting reflective tape or stickers on the frame. Cover the frame's chips and scratches with paint that doesn't match.

Announce your route. When you're heading out for a ride, it doesn't hurt to tell a friend or roommate where you're going and when you'll be back. Then they'll know where to start looking if you don't return on time.

Stay alert. Avoid roads and trails where you know threats or attacks have occurred. Watch out for suspicious characters near debris in the road. Stick to main streets, avoiding alleys and cramped, bad neighborhoods. Talk to other cyclists and keep up with community news. Above all, vary the time and route you ride, which lessens your chance of being picked out as a target.

Listen to yourself. Your instincts and perceptions are invaluable when it comes to personal survival, says Gavin de Becker in his book *The Gift of Fear*. If the guy standing on the street corner up ahead is making you uneasy, don't second-guess your feelings. There's probably a reason. Trust your inner self and turn around. Don't worry about hurting the feelings of someone you don't even know. Don't analyze your fear or discomfort, just heed it.

If Trouble Happens

Keep rolling if someone starts hassling you. You have two big advantages on a bicycle: You're more mobile than a car and faster than someone on foot, points out Crystal Nelson, a Nashville bike patrol police officer. In an iffy situation, stay on your bike and keep moving. "Don't give up your mechanical advantage," Nelson says. Sure, if someone wants just your bike, it may be best to hand it over, but you can't know what anyone really has in mind.

Plan an escape route. Pick out escape routes ahead of time, advises Glowacz. If someone seems to be following you, think ahead and turn into a busy street, a storefront, or even someone's driveway. Don't automatically stop for a flat tire should it happen in a weird setting. Sometimes it's better to risk trashing the tire and rim by riding a ways to a safer place.

Call for help. A cell phone, programmed to speed-dial local authorities or 911, can let others know about a problem in seconds. A potential assailant may head the other way when he sees you using it.

Fight back. Ditch the concept that good girls don't get into trouble—fight back with every ounce of energy you have. Hold your bike between you and your would-be attacker, then shove it at him and run in the opposite direction, says Glowacz. Scream, kick, gouge, hit. Bad guys want quiet victims, so don't be one. If you're being dragged, collapse to make it more difficult. Some people like to carry pepper spray, but check to make sure it's legal in your state. Attach the canister to your clothing rather than your bike, so it stays with you; and practice using it ahead of time.

Go to Class

Better bike-handling skills make for a safer and more confident cyclist who is better equipped to handle threatening situations. Sign up for an Effective Cycling class through the League of American Bicyclists (www.bikeleague.org). Jacquie Phelan, former mountain bike racer and founder of WOMBATS (Women's Mountain Bike and Tea Society), recommends mountain bike classes to increase off-road riding skills and lessen the chance of injury. Check the WOMBATS Web site at www.wombats.org.

4

Street Savvy

BY SUSAN SORENSEN

My first bicycle, a blue Schwinn with a basket and bell, was a gift for my sixth birthday. Once I overcame my fear of tipping over, I gave little thought to safety. And as long as I had a rubber band to keep my bell-bottoms from catching in the chain, my attire scarcely mattered.

Cycling has come a long way since then. Today's bicycles, better and faster, certainly aren't just for kids. In fact, the Bicycle Federation of America tells us that there now are more adults than children riding bikes. This doesn't mean, however, that we all have a grown-up understanding of the core rules of smart cycling. If you're getting back on a bike after a few years away, you may remember your mother or father yelling some of these same things as you wobbled down the driveway. Only then, you were too excited to listen closely and in too much of a youthful hurry to ask why.

Ride with traffic. Although it might seem safer to go like walkers and runners and ride against the flow of traffic so you can see approaching vehicles, nothing is more dangerous. There are three reasons.

First, it's confusing to motorists, especially at intersections where, for example, they aren't conditioned to look for vehicles approaching from the right when making a right turn. This is also why riding the wrong way on a one-way street is so risky.

Second, consider the physics. Let's say a car is going 40 mph and you're pedaling at 15 mph. If you're riding against traffic, you approach each other at 55 mph. But if you're riding with traffic, the car overtakes you at only 25 mph. The driver has more time to think and respond.

Third, you're actually breaking the law if you ride against traffic. In all states, cyclists are legally required to follow the same traffic rules as motor vehicles.

Signal your turns. Before changing lanes or turning, indicate your intention to motorists and other cyclists. It's easy to indicate a left turn—just extend your left arm. For a right turn, most cycling experts agree that your intention is clearer if you extend your right arm, not hold your left arm up as a driver would. (The latter practice began because drivers simply can't point a right turn with their right arm.) But either way is acceptable. To indicate that you're stopping, hold your left arm down with your palm facing rearward. If cyclists are close behind, it's easier and faster to say "Stopping!" loud enough to be heard clearly.

Behave predictably. Don't zip in and out of traffic or weave in and out among cars parked parallel along the street. Riding in a fairly straight, predictable line gives drivers confidence in you and may keep them from making a mistake in judgment as they attempt to pass.

Don't run stop signs, dart from street to sidewalk and back, or unnecessarily hinder traffic at intersections by blocking the turning lane. For instance, if the law permits a right turn on red but you're going straight, stop just on the inside of the straight-ahead lane so cars can pass on your right to turn.

Be careful when cycling past cars that are parallel parked. A door could suddenly open in your path, causing a nasty crash. Watch through rear windows, and if someone is sitting on the left side, ride far enough into the traffic lane to miss the door if it should suddenly open. If you establish this distance and maintain a steady line, drivers may not like the fact that you're in the road but they can deal with it.

In general, think of the behavior that irritates you most about cyclists when you're driving, and avoid those actions. If you respect the rules of the road and the rights of motorists, they are more likely to respect you.

Choose your route wisely. If you do just a little planning, you can almost always get from here to there on streets that are less congested. As your bike-handling skill and confidence improve, route selection may matter less. But as a developing rider, make things easier on yourself by using lightly traveled back streets rather than busy arterial roads. Buy a city map so you can plot alternate routes that you never considered using as a driver.

Be seen. Loud colors may not be your usual style, but on a bike you want to make sure you're seen by motorists. Wear a bright red, pink, yellow, or orange shirt or jersey. Tests show that in broad daylight, hot colors are spotted much more easily at a distance than dark hues such as blue, green, or brown. The disparity is even greater on a cloudy or rainy day. Helmets come in vibrant colors, too.

For riding in low-light conditions or in the dark, wear white and have lots of reflective material on your bike and body. Reflective fabrics or strips on clothing help to show you as a human form in the darkness. Reflective bands worn around your ankles attract drivers' attention as your feet bob up and down during pedaling. The law says you must have front and rear lights, too. In the city, where there are streetlights to help you see the road, point your front light up a bit so it's more likely to catch the eyes of drivers.

Think ahead. Anticipate the actions of motorists. Analyze traffic situations and ride defensively, just as you do when driving. One trick is to look drivers directly in the eye at intersections. This will tell you if they're daydreaming or if they know you're there. Also, take note of a stopped driver's wheels as you approach an intersection. If they're rolling slightly, he may be about to pull out in front of you. If they're angled, he's probably going to turn even if his turn signal isn't on. Similarly, never pull out in front of a vehicle because it's blinking for a turn. The driver could have left the signal on by mistake.

Use your ears, too. Listen for vehicles coming up from behind. With practice, you'll even be able to gauge how close they may come. Never wear earphones, because they rob you of this valuable protection. In fact, they're illegal for cycling in some states.

Don't, however, rely solely on your ears to tell you whether there's a car behind you. Always look behind before changing lanes or pulling into traffic. To do this, develop the skill of pedaling in a straight line while glancing back over your shoulder. It's common to swerve by unintentionally turning the handlebar when you turn your head, so practice in an empty parking lot away from traffic. It helps to pivot your shoulders first, stabilize, then pivot your head. Soon, this will be second nature.

Some riders like to keep tabs on what's behind by using a rearview mirror. There are various styles that attach to your handlebar, helmet, or glasses. Mirrors are effective but not foolproof—their field of vision is small and contains blind spots. Always double-check by glancing back before moving into the traffic flow.

Don't overreact to incidents. In this age of road rage, it's dangerous to incite drivers. You can't win a fight when you're on a bicycle and they're in 3,000-pound motorized machines (with who knows what under the seats). Should a motorist cut you off or yell something at you, it's always going to be tempting to shout back or throw up a finger. Don't. Let it go and it will quickly be over. React and the result could be a problem that affects you for a long time. Of course, a truly hostile action should be reported to the police, so get the license number or at least a description of the vehicle.

Handling Harassment

Do you fear harassment on the road? Many women do. A rude slap, shout, or horn blast is more than disconcerting, it's dangerous. It could cause you to swerve, lose control, and crash. Even worse are offenders who throw bottles or other objects or even try to force you off the road. It doesn't help much to know that male cyclists suffer the same indignities. We feel vulnerable once it has happened to us.

The first time I ever had my rump thumped, I was too outraged and surprised to do anything but shout in anger. The next time, I wrote down the license plate number. When I called the police, they refused to reprimand the driver unless I was willing to press charges. I didn't want to retaliate, I just wanted to make the offender think. So I dropped the matter.

How do we stop this sort of thing and keep it from intimidating us? Patti Brehler, a cyclist from Michigan, told me about the arsenal of responses she has developed.

As she points out, the harasser just wants to get a reaction. "So when it used to happen, I'd call, 'I love you!' instead of flipping them off. Laugh it off," she advises. "You don't solve anything by getting upset; you just stress yourself."

Brehler says that by improving her cycling skills, she made herself a less vulnerable-looking target. If you feel

Don't let socializing interfere with safety. When you stop to regroup with your friends or read a map, pull well off the road. Avoid taking a break just over the crest of a hill or around a curve, where drivers won't see you ahead of time.

In most states, you have the legal right to ride two abreast, but don't be obstinate about it. Switch to single file on a busy road so drivers won't back up, get frustrated, then veer dangerously around you. If a line of cars forms anyway, pull over briefly to let them pass. In this case, a group of cyclists should split into smaller bunches of three or four. Leave a few car lengths between these subgroups to aid passing cars. Being considerate does much to further goodwill on the road.

Wear a helmet. I know, you never wore a helmet as a kid and you took your share of spills without cracking your skull. Consider, however, that 1,000 people die every year from cycling accidents, and most of these fatalities stem from head trauma. Accident statistics show that helmets can reduce the risk of head injury by nearly 80 percent.

confident and project that, it makes a difference. "If women can take care of themselves, it shows," she says.

Good cycling skills offer another benefit. When you ride like a driver, motorists don't have to deviate from obeying traffic laws to accommodate you. Also, when someone behind the wheel is doing something unusual, it's easier to spot. Then you can take action sooner.

Brehler finds that it helps to wear a rearview mirror on her helmet. "There have been times I've gotten off the road because I thought I'd better. Either the car looked like it was trying to get too close, or I saw that arm out the window."

Sometimes, dress can be a factor. Brehler generally avoids halter tops or short crop tops, plus anything that's going to show cleavage as she leans over the bar. A helmet, in addition to its protection, helps disguise gender.

How much should you worry about harassment? I've talked with many women who experience little trouble. The problem seems to vary from one region to another and even between populated and rural areas within a region. Any cyclist—female or male—can expect an incident every now and then. That's reality, but don't let it stop you from enjoying all of the positive aspects of cycling.

By Susan Weaver

Take into account, too, that you're riding in a much different fashion from when you were a kid on a small bike. Your head, higher from the ground, will impact with greater force. Your speed is faster and you're in more traffic, too. Modern helmets are light, airy, and stylish—and mandatory for most organized events. So get used to wearing one every time you ride. Before long, you'll feel naked without it.

Prevent bike theft. If you must leave your pride and joy where you can't keep an eye on it, secure it to a strong, stationary object such as a parking meter or metal fence. There are many types of locks, depending on the level of security you need. But no matter which type you use, the technique is the same: Enclose your bike's seat tube and both wheels in the lock (so a wheel can't be stolen). To do this, you may have to remove the front wheel by opening its quick-release, then set it next to the rear wheel.

5
After the Fall

BY ROBIN STUART

If you ride a bike, it will happen to you. It doesn't matter whether your tires are smooth or knobby, if you ride once a week or every day, or if you ride alone or in groups: It will happen to you. You may even have learned how to do it in a way that keeps the damage to a minimum, secretly believing that as long as you are cautious, you will never be called on to perform the technique.

And then, when you least suspect it, it happens. To you. One minute, you're enjoying the great outdoors, and the next, your blood is mixed with dirt or asphalt in bicycling's baptism.

As a writer and teacher of things treadular, I'm often asked to speak on behalf of my gender as to the greatest difference between women and men. Although I usually balk at generalizations that include more than 20 million people, after much contemplation, I think I've come up with at least one real answer: crashing.

Most of the differences are so obvious that they become moot. Physical structure and physiological distinctions have been bandied about ad nauseam. "Muscle mass, blah, blah, blah. Fat cells, blah, blah, blah. Pelvic bones, blah, blah, blah." You want to know what truly divides the sexes? Simple psychology. Women think differently than men. Women are more afraid of crashes.

Before all those hard-core, my-scars-are-bigger-than-his-scars gals start warming up their fax machines and home computers to lambaste this appraisal, let me just add that it's a question of degrees. Some women are more afraid than others, and some types of crashes frighten us more than others. The fact remains, however, that we seem to think about it more than guys.

How did I arrive at this revelation? Aside from my personal experiences with ultra-sensitivity to Earth's gravitational pull, it's based on the questions I've heard in my all-women classes and from neophyte female friends. The most popular one is a two-parter: "What about crashing? Does it hurt?" I can't recall any male acquaintances voicing similar concerns.

In responding to students and comrades alike, I try to sound as chipper as possible while visibly horrifying them with the truth: "Sometimes."

Still on the fence? Flip your channel to ESPN and watch a downhill mountain bike race. I did this one day in 1996. There was Jimmy Deaton tearing down a mountain wearing his teeny-tiny knee pads better suited to light carpentry. There was Dave Cullinan with his cute little Kevlar knee- and shin-guard cutouts sewn tastefully into his spandex pants below his team jersey. Then I saw (barely) Kim Sonier beneath her layers of body armor. And who was that looking like one of the Teenage Mutant Ninja Turtles, all plastic joints and webbed ventilators? Oh, Regina Stiefl.

Yeah, sure, you're thinking. What about Missy Giove? She's a woman and she's not afraid to crash.

Correction: Missy is not afraid of anything.

Please don't think I'm passing judgment—I'm merely stating an observation. I've talked to many women, and been there myself, and the one common theme is our hyperawareness of terra firma and its hold over us, or under us, as the case may be.

But it's not such a bad thing. After all, realizing your fear holds the key to its resolution. The very nature of our chosen sport is to guide us on a collision course, so to speak, to our own enlightenment and ultimate freedom. Girls and women everywhere are being liberated daily, forced to face their fears by the occasional pratfall into a thorn bush or knee skid on a sidewalk. Why, as you read this, there's probably a woman examining a new flesh wound somewhere in the world, regarding her torn skin with a mixture of pain and pride.

To this woman, and all of us like her, I say, "Celebrate." Use the experience, learn from it, and most important, become a better rider because of it. Respect your chosen terrain but try not to fear it. Revel in the knowledge that the next time your biking buddies compare battle scars, you'll have something to bring to the table. If you scraped a leg, wear shorts. If you banged up an elbow, wear T-shirts. Be proud. It happened, and yet you survived.

But I am a woman. I have to give in to my feminine nature and add: Ride within your abilities, and always wear your helmet.

PART TWO

Made for Women

6
Breaking the Bounds

BY ELLEN GARVEY

The increasing quantity of cycling products specially designed for women—short-reach brake levers, seats, helmets, shorts, jerseys, frames with compact top tubes—is encouraging. But if you think that such products are something new, think again.

Cycling equipment created just for women has been around about as long as women have been riding bikes. But unlike the modern stuff, which is designed to improve our performance, those first products were meant to keep women's riding within bounds and deflect criticism of it. It's a fascinating and mostly unknown story.

Bicycling for women lofted onto the scene in the 1890s. Until then, bicycles were relatively dangerous high-wheel models, ridden almost exclusively by athletic young men. With the development of the "safety" bicycle (which had wheels of equal size, a chain drive, and air-filled tires), cycling became more accessible. Women, who already had abundant motives to move beyond their chaperoned and constricted lives, seized the opportunity to ride.

Women's rights advocates were ecstatic. Cycling became more than just a way to get out and about. Feminists exulted that the bicycle would force dress reform—allowing them to go uncorseted and wear divided skirts or bloomers—and believed that once women commanded such physical freedom they could surely throw off other oppressive constraints. Suffragist and temperance leader Frances Willard, who learned to ride at age 53, called her bicycle an "implement of power."

Where women saw liberation, conservatives saw a threat. They claimed that "mannish" cycling women, caricatured as strutting and smoking cigars, would ride beyond social controls and either refuse marriage or become so sexually loose that they'd be unmarriable.

Sex in the Saddle
The oddest form of assault on women's riding was an outpouring of dozens of medical articles that attacked cycling not only as likely to make women masculine but also as a threat to sexual purity. As one

doctor wrote, "The saddle can be tilted in every bicycle as desired. . . . In this way a girl . . . could, by carrying the front peak or pommel high, or by relaxing the stretched leather in order to let it form a deep, hammock-like concavity which would fit itself snugly over the entire vulva and reach up in front, bring about constant friction over the clitoris and labia. This pressure would be much increased by stooping forward, and the warmth generated from vigorous exercise might further increase the feeling."

It gets stranger. To bike makers, opposition to women's cycling was an obstacle to sales. So manufacturers addressed the "problem" with a doggedly concrete and literal solution: modified seats that eliminated contact with genitals.

Ad copy for these "hygienic" seats typically warned of the "injurious" or "harmful pressure exerted by other saddles," carried medical endorsements, or declared their saddles free of "pressure against sensitive parts"—all euphemisms drawn from medical writing. (I find it somewhat ironic that modern versions of the split-seat and soft-nose designs are now targeted at men suffering from cycling-related urinary, numbness, or erection problems.)

The "stooping forward" posture that our good doctor objected to was the position adopted by "scorchers," or the fastest riders. Speed was seen as dreadfully inappropriate for women—it let them roam even farther—so speed was specifically linked to saddle masturbation. For instance, another physician complained that "the moment speed is desired the body is bent forward in a characteristic curve . . . [and] the body is thrown forward, causing the clothing to press again the clitoris, thereby eliciting and arousing feelings hitherto unknown and unrealized by the young maiden."

Scorching also meant abandoning the ideal of graceful upright riding that articles and manuals urged women to attain. Companies had to show that there was a masculine (scorching) and feminine (upright) way to ride. Adjustments to promote feminine riding were common. One cycling manual made scorching impossible for women by recommending that the handlebar be positioned 2 to 3 inches higher than the saddle for a man, but 4 to 5 inches above the saddle for a woman.

Despite these barriers, women continued pushing the boundaries of cycling. Just as they do in our era, bikes offered too much escape and independence to ignore.

7
Perfect Match

BY THE EDITORS OF *BICYCLING* MAGAZINE

Thinking of buying a new or used bike? Want to check whether your present bike is exactly right for you? Because there are several distinct types of bike, let's narrow it down by answering these basic questions.

What type of cycling do you want to do? Do you want to join in the group rides of the local bike club? Does racing appeal to you? Or maybe tooling around town on two wheels seems more practical and fun than gridlock and parking decks. Do you picture yourself pedaling a mountain bike along secluded forest trails or seeing the country from the seat of a touring bike? Perhaps you want a fresh-air alternative to long lines at the health club.

Whatever your main riding interest, talk with some like-minded cyclists about the types of bikes and equipment that work for them. You can meet these riders through local bike shops or clubs or just by introducing yourself when you meet someone during a ride. Show interest in their bikes, and maybe they'll even let you give theirs a try.

Meanwhile, to meet your needs, think through these questions: Where will you ride? Are you blessed with miles of scenic, lightly traveled paved roads? Is there a network of trails waiting to be explored? How about safe bike lanes for traveling on city streets? You'll ride more and heighten your cycling enjoyment if you own a bike that lets you take advantage of your area's best opportunities.

All Kinds of Bikes

An efficient racing or sport touring bike is best for the road. To ride unpaved trails, you need a mountain bike. For combining pavement with packed dirt or gravel, choose a bike that mixes features of a road and mountain bike. These are called hybrids or cross bikes. For urban commuting, mountain bikes and hybrids are popular, but a road bike will work well if it has beefy tires and wheels to reduce the risks from broken pavement and glass. For casual recreational riding, perhaps on bike paths or in parks where there are no big hills, consider a comfort bike or cruiser. These recent additions to the lineup give you an upright riding position and other easy-pedaling features. They simplify shifting by having either just one speed or the convenience and reliability of several gears inside the rear hub. These aren't performance bikes, but they're fine for casual riding.

Will you ride with a group? If not, the slower speed of a mountain bike or hybrid on pavement may be tolerable. But trying to keep pace with others on road bikes when you're pumping the pedals of a slower-accelerating, fat-tire bike could discourage you from group riding altogether.

Do you need carrying capacity? High-performance road and mountain bikes usually don't have fittings on the frames for attaching racks. They also may not have the stable handling required to tote heavy loads. If you haul more gear than will fit in a large seatbag, make sure your bike's frame has rack fittings (called dropout eyelets). Then you can attach a rack and fasten a rack trunk on top, or even use front and rear panniers (large bags that fit beside the wheels). Panniers give you enough capacity for groceries or all of the gear you'll need for a tour.

How fit are you? If you're already in shape for cycling, you can probably handle the higher, more closely spaced gears of a road racing bike. If you're not that fit but your goal is to get strong on the road, a racing or sport touring bike is still appropriate if it has a moderate gear range. To handle big hills and still have a sporty road bike, look into one with a three-chainring crankset (called a triple). The third chainring produces very low gears similar to those found on mountain bikes and hybrids.

By the way, don't be misled by the term "racing bike." Most racing bike riders, like most sports car owners, don't compete. With few exceptions, a racing bike requires no more skill to ride than a recreational model and is scarcely less comfortable. Its advantage is lighter weight and greater efficiency, helping a reasonably fit cyclist cover more ground more quickly.

If riding hard and fast is less important to you than versatility, a hybrid is a good choice. It will even work for loaded touring, though you may want to add bar-ends to its flat handlebar so you'll have more hand positions when riding long distances. If you buy a mountain bike, you'll ride slower because of its greater weight and the extra rolling resistance of its knobby tires. On the other hand, you'll have plenty of easy-pedaling low gears. These are necessary for the steep hills typical of off-road riding. You need these gears even if you're racer-fit.

Are you fascinated by technology? Some riders crave the cachet and aerodynamic advantages of high-performance bicycles. If your riding style is equally competitive, own the most advanced bike you can afford. In the long run, it's more expensive to buy a lesser bike and upgrade its parts later.

How devoted a cyclist will you be? A big-bucks road or mountain bike designed for competition is overkill if you're just pedaling casually on your local bike path on weekends. But if you expect cycling to become an increasingly important part of your life, go ahead and get a better bike than your current fitness or skill requires. Thus, as you continue to improve as a rider, you'll still own a suitable machine. Often, riders thwart their development because they underestimate their riding potential and buy an inadequate bike. They fail to see their purchase as an investment in a lifelong sport.

Are you looking for something outside the norm? If by now you're saying, "None of the above," you may be a candidate for a recumbent (it's easy on the back and the backside) or even a tandem (if you plan to ride frequently with another person). Or if you think they just don't make bikes like they used to, check out a one-speed cruiser for casual, uh, cruising.

Do your cycling interests cross all boundaries? Considering how specialized bicycles can be, you may wish—like many enthusiasts—to have two bikes (perhaps one for road riding and one for unpaved trails) instead of compromising on one. It's a matter of having the right tool for the job. A hybrid can work for either surface, but it will not be as efficient on pavement as a pure road bike or nearly as competent on dirt as a pure mountain bike. Many bike shops are seeing customers who bought a mountain bike for all-purpose use coming back to buy a road bike or a hybrid.

Dollars and Sense

The first step in making a good bike buy is to avoid department store disappointments. In the cycling industry, profit margins are narrow, so you get what you pay for. At bike shops, you'll find high-quality products and skilled personnel to help you with your selection. Expect to spend at least $300 for a reliable, no-frills, entry-level bicycle. Every additional $100 you can afford will buy an increasingly better frame or components, up to around $1,000, at which point extra money means more and more subtle refinements.

Speaking of budgets, if you're just getting into cycling, remember to allow for the cost of necessary accessories. These include a helmet ($30 to $130), frame pump ($20 to $50), spare tube and patch kit ($15), seatbag ($10 to $20), and water bottle and cage ($7 to $20). You can usually save if you buy these as a package deal when purchasing a bike from a shop. Also important are cycling shorts with a soft, absorbent, lightly padded liner ($25 to $75).

Certainly, the most popular bikes during the 1990s have been mountain bikes. This brings up the question of suspension and whether it's worth paying extra for. The difference between riding a conventional unsuspended bike, a front-suspension bike, and a bike with front and rear suspension is similar to the difference between jumping off your porch with your knees locked versus jumping onto one leg with your knee bent versus jumping with both knees bent. With bent knees, the muscles in your legs act like springs that absorb the energy of the impact. Now, imagining your legs as springs, transfer that image to the suspension on a bike.

Actually, it's becoming difficult to find a new mountain bike that lacks front suspension. Rigid forks have all but disappeared as the cost of shock-absorbing forks has dropped. So the question now facing most mountain bike shoppers is whether to get a model that has a rear shock absorber, too. A bike built with both front and rear suspension is said to have dual suspension.

The good news is that the starting price of dual-suspension bikes has dropped to below $1,000. Still, this may not be a bargain if the type of terrain you ride doesn't justify the extra weight and complexity of rear suspension. Because dual-suspension bikes are heavier, you have to work harder to ride them up hills, and some designs waste a bit of pedaling effort by flexing as your legs push down. A lighter and less expensive alternative that takes the bite out of big bumps is a shock-absorbing seatpost. Installing one can turn any bike with a suspension fork into an effective dual-suspension machine. Don't forget, though, that simply by getting your buttocks off the seat and keeping your elbows and knees flexed, your body can provide its own dual suspension.

Size Wise

Whether you're evaluating the fit of a possible purchase or evaluating the suitability of your present bike, you need to determine your proper frame size. Vertically, this is done by measuring "standover"—the clearance between your crotch and the top tube when you straddle the bike while wearing your riding shoes. Depending on the type of bike and how you'll be using it, you should have at least 2 inches of clearance.

It's usually easy to find a bike that fits your legs. The tricky part is making sure it also fits your torso. Horizontally, bikes tend to stretch women too much. This is because most bikes are designed to fit men, who have proportionately longer torsos and arms compared to their overall height than women do. This effect seems especially exaggerated for women who are 5 foot 4 or shorter. Be sure the combined length of the top tube and stem (called reach) is not too rangy for your comfort.

If you've decided that a hybrid is right for you, good fit will be easier to achieve because of the more upright sitting position that this bike allows. Meanwhile, finding a road or mountain bike with correct reach has been made easier by the increasing availability of bikes proportioned for women.

Critical Components

Proportioned bicycles should come with in-scale components. Even if a standard frame fits your legs and torso, you may be more comfortable after adjusting things such as brake levers or handlebar width. If you are updating an older bike, look into switching to women-specific components. They could end years of compromised comfort. Here's an overview of components to consider. You'll find more detail in the remaining chapters of this section.

Saddle. Women's pelvises are slightly wider than men's. To support the sit bones (and keep weight from resting solely on the genitalia), women generally need saddles that are a little wider in the rear than those that guys require. You'll find several so-called anatomical seats for women at bike shops. Some women have no trouble with the standard seats that came on their bikes. But if you feel that your seat just isn't right, try some anatomical models. Try to take test-rides in order to find the one that fits you best. It's hard to tell just by sitting on seats in the shop, and you can't go by recommendations of friends or salespeople, because everyone is different.

Stem. You can compensate for a longish top tube by installing a shorter stem, which brings the handlebar closer. But first try the simplest fix: Raise the stem you have, which positions the bar higher and a bit closer. (Be sure not to raise the stem past its maximum-extension line, or so high that you create an awkward riding position.)

Handlebar. Women also differ from men in shoulder width. Women are generally narrower, so a bar may spread the arms and cause shoulder, upper-back, and neck pain. This also compromises bike handling. In general, the length of a handlebar should match your shoulder width (measured to the bony ends of your shoulders). For a road bike, consider a drop handlebar such as the Terry T-Bar, which comes as narrow as 36 cm and also has indentations that bring the brake levers closer to your hands.

On mountain bikes, you can have the handlebar shortened with a pipe cutter at any bike shop.

Brake levers. On a mountain bike, you should be able to easily reach and pull the brake levers with just your first two fingers on each hand. If your hands feel too stretched, your levers are too far away. Many mountain bike brake systems have adjustment screws that position the levers closer to the bar.

On a road bike, try braking from atop the brake hoods. If you can't exert enough force to come quickly to a full stop, the levers aren't sized for you and won't let you ride safely using this comfortable hand position. Bike shops can install short-reach road levers for you.

8
Do You Need a Women's Bike?

BY SARA J. HENRY

When I started riding, there wasn't much to bike sizing. You bought any frame that wasn't too big to stand over. You rode bent way forward like the guys, and if it hurt, well, it hurt. Eventually, I switched to a shorter stem to ease the ache in my back, but that was the only concession I made. When other female riders complained of seat or neck or shoulder pain, I thought *What wimps!* and told them, "You'll get used to it."

Some did and some didn't. I was lucky. I was tall, with long arms and slim hips, so my bike fit better than most women's. But all women aren't built alike—and we're not built like men. Most women have proportionately shorter torsos and longer legs than men, plus wider pelvises and less upper-body strength, according to Andrew Pruitt, Ed.D., director of Boulder Center for Sports Medicine in Colorado. Dr. Pruitt knows cyclists and their fitting problems because he has worked for years with U.S. national team riders at the Olympic Training Center in Colorado Springs. Even if a bike fits a woman's leg length, its top tube, stem, or crankarms may be too long and its saddle could be too narrow.

So what happens if your bike doesn't fit right? If you ride only a couple of miles around the neighborhood, probably nothing, says Dr. Pruitt. But if you crank up the mileage, you can experience back, neck, hip, or butt pain in varying degrees of severity. And your pedaling efficiency can suffer just as much. Thankfully, these problems are now well-understood, and more manufacturers are answering the need for bikes that fit women better. These are some of their considerations.

1. Frame. Because of their proportionately shorter torsos, women usually need shorter top tubes. But if the rider is quite small—say, under 5 foot 4—the top tube can be so short that it brings the front wheel too close. This causes the feet to overlap the wheel when either one is fully forward in the pedal stroke. The result can be contact and a crash during slow riding, when the wheel may be turned sharply. Some manufacturers resolve this problem by using a smaller-diameter front wheel. Georgena Terry, founder of Terry Precision Cycling for Women, is a leader in this area. Her company makes its smaller road bikes with a 24-inch front wheel and a standard 700C wheel in back. This trick also allows these bikes to retain a relatively normal head-tube angle for proper steering behavior.

It's also important to have the correct seat angle to ensure that your saddle (and subsequently your legs) is in the correct fore/aft position above the crankset. (Moving your saddle back and forth enables you to fine-tune this.) Generally, people with longer thighs need a 72- or 73-degree seat angle, and shorter-thighed folks do better with a slightly steeper angle that moves them farther forward over the crankset.

2. Stem. The oldest trick in the book is to compensate for an overly long top tube by installing a stem with a shorter forward extension. This brings the handlebar closer to the saddle. Several manufacturers make very short stems. Your local bike shop can order one for you if they're not in stock.

3. Handlebar. Women's shoulders tend to be narrower then men's. A bar that's right for a guy may be too wide for you and cause pain in the shoulders, upper back, and neck. Terry offers 36- and 38-cm drop-style road handlebars to more precisely correspond to a woman's shoulder width (measured from bony end to bony end). Most flat handlebars found on mountain bikes and hybrids can easily be shortened with a pipe cutter at a bike shop.

4. Crankarms. Look on the back of the arms and you'll see a number stamped in the metal. Arm lengths of 160 or 165 mm, rather than the standard 170 mm, are a better fit for women (and men) who have an inseam of less than 29½ inches (measured from crotch to floor in bare feet). Keep in mind that mountain bike crankarms should be 5 mm longer than those on road bikes. The extra length gives you better leverage for steep climbs and slow-speed maneuvers. So the best size for your mountain bike will probably be 170 mm.

5. Saddle. Because women's pelvises are slightly wider than men's, the part of the pelvic bones we sit on (the ischial tuberosities) are farther apart. To support these bones and keep weight from resting solely

on our genitalia, we generally need saddles that are a little wider in the rear. You can usually find these so-called anatomical saddles in stock at your local shop, because sooner or later, many women want them in their quests for greater comfort.

6. Brake levers. With smaller hands and shorter fingers, many women can benefit from short-reach brake levers for their road bikes. Check at a shop for the models currently available. Usually, mountain bike levers don't need to be replaced, because most have adjustment screws that let you shorten their distance to the bar.

The Bottom Line

So, with all of these component options to alter an off-the-rack bike, do you really need one that's designed from scratch for women? Some women like me—5 foot 9 with long arms—can do fine on a standard frame as long as the top tube is at the short end of the size range. Racers and triathletes striving for the most streamlined position are likely to prefer a bike that stretches them out more. You can adjust any bike to fit better as long as the standover height is correct (about 2 inches for a road bike; at least 3 inches for a mountain bike). You can get a shorter stem and wider saddle. You can move the saddle forward a bit and tilt the handlebar up. You can install shorter crankarms and shorter-reach brake levers, or a taller stem that lets you sit more upright.

But trade-offs exist. A saddle shoved too far forward can cause ineffi-cient pedaling and knee problems. A very short stem can result in squir-relly bike handling—as I learned when I switched to a bike with a shorter top tube and longer stem and discovered that I wasn't the rotten bike handler I had thought I was. If your bike setup is maxed out, you may not be able to make additional adjustments should your cycling style change. And for some women, all the adjustments in the world to standard bikes won't make their discomfort disappear.

Also, there are real advantages to getting a bike that is designed for women. For example, several major manufacturers offer models engi-neered specifically for the women most likely to have serious problems fitting on standard bikes—those under 5 foot 4. Bike models change every year, so check at shops to see what is currently available for women in the brands they carry.

Georgena Terry has built her women's cycling business by offering bikes that fit women from 4 foot 10 to 5 foot 11, not just those under 5 foot 4. No matter how tall a woman is, she notes, "her muscles are not only generally smaller than a man's but are also distributed differently, resulting in more force on joints. A slightly more upright riding position eases those forces."

No, not every woman needs a women's bike. But every woman needs a bike that fits, particularly in the critical distance between the saddle and handlebar. A woman's bike may be the best place to start looking.

9
Have a Seat

BY CARLOTTA CUERDON

Women have spent years on hard, narrow saddles designed with no regard for the female anatomy. Fortunately, manufacturers now understand that we are shaped differently than men (surprise!). Because we have wider, shallower pelvises, we can benefit from saddles with shorter noses and wider rear sections.

Avocet, a California company, started the revolution in saddle technology with the introduction of an "anatomic" seat back in 1977. One longtime user told me, "It was the first truly comfortable seat I'd ever used. It changed my whole attitude toward riding." She's still using that seat today. Many other women also discovered how much more pleasurable cycling can be on a saddle that fits, creating success for Avocet and inspiring other companies to design models for the female market. The result is numerous shorter, wider seats with features such as gel inserts or even holes through the top to lessen pressure on tender body parts.

Saddle contact occurs in three places: two in the rear, where your ischial tuberosities ("sit bones") support most of your weight; and up front where your pudendum (the soft, external genitalia) rests on the saddle nose. Because women are built for bearing children, our pelvises are shaped in a way that puts our sit bones farther apart. If a saddle isn't wide enough, these bones fall outside the sitting surface and much more weight rests on the soft tissue between them. Finding a seat that's wide enough to fully support your sit bones is the key factor in the selection process.

Here's a way to get a sense of your sit-bone width and how they feel when in full contact with something. Simply squat down and sit on a curb. In this position, your sit bones are prominent and easily felt through your butt's soft padding. A saddle should be wide enough to support them in a similar way.

Women's pelvises also tend to tilt forward, putting weight on their pudenda. For this reason, it helps to have a saddle with a shorter, well-padded nose. Then it must be positioned correctly, with the top hori-

Saddle Softeners

You've chosen a saddle that fits your anatomy, and your riding position is on the money. But your comfort still isn't what you'd like it to be, especially when you're traveling on rough roads or trails. You're a good candidate for a product that is gaining favor with many cyclists—a shock-absorbing seatpost. It's an effective and relatively affordable ($60 and up) way to add rear suspension to any bike. There are two basic types.

The simpler design looks much like a regular seatpost. It contains elastomers or a spring and slides up and down in line with the bike's bottom bracket. This works, but it has the disadvantage of changing your seat height as you ride over big bumps (more of a concern off-road than on). Also, because your weight isn't always centered on the saddle, the forces applied to the post aren't always in line with its movement. This increases friction and wear, possibly resulting in looseness over time.

The other type is more complex, which makes it heavier and more costly, but most riders agree that it also works better. Atop this post is a parallelogram, a four-bar linkage that absorbs bumps by moving the saddle more horizontally than vertically. It makes sort of an arc, relative to the bottom bracket. This keeps your saddle's height quite constant, though it does vary its distance to the handlebar. The amount is too small to notice (or at least make a difference) for most riders.

How effective are these devices? According to pro racer Ned Overend in his book *Mountain Bike like a Champion*, "I put a suspension seatpost on my wife's bike. It made a ton of difference to her enjoyment because she doesn't ride enough to develop great technique. Now she no longer fears being pounded by the saddle."

zontal or tilted nose-down just a degree or two. Be careful—greater tilt may cause you to lean too far forward, putting uncomfortable pressure on your hands and arms. To judge tilt, set your bike against a wall and lay a yardstick lengthwise along the center of the seat. Stand back to see if the yardstick is horizontal with the ground or tilted in either direction. Saddle height and other elements of correct position are essential for comfort, too, so carefully follow the guidelines in chapters 11 and 12.

Choice Seating

Saddle models come and go, so it's possible that some seats mentioned here may have been replaced by even better designs when you read this book. Prices also can change. Check at your local bike shops to see what is current. Ask for permission to test-ride any saddle before you buy, or get a 30-day satisfaction guarantee.

The following saddles are far from the only ones designed for women, but as I write this in 1999, they represent some of the newest or most innovative. Subjective comments are compiled from several women, including myself, who tested these saddles for *Bicycling* magazine. By reading about these saddles, you'll pick up tips for choosing the best one for yourself.

Mountain Bike Saddles

Avocet X-Country Women's. This pioneer company's latest line of women's saddles includes this one, which is an inch wider than its racing model. The broader rear with ample padding offers comfortable support for the sit bones. The sides ("hips") are squared off and reinforced with carbon fiber, providing a place to push against with your thighs when bike-handling in tricky terrain. The rear slopes down to help you slide off and on. This saddle should please the recreational off-road rider, while racers may want something trimmer and lighter. Weight with leather cover and titanium rails is 260 grams. $99.

Selle San Marco Race Day. Judging from the name, you can guess that this saddle is meant for racers. It's available in slightly different versions that are named after former world champions Juli Furtado or Paola Pezzo. The Race Day has lopped-off hips, making it great for technical terrain—easy to get behind and to grip and steer with your thighs. Its slightly down-turned nose helps prevent shorts from getting snagged, and the top padding does a good job of cushioning bumps on the trail. There's an oval gel insert right where you roll forward on your pudendum. Weight with leather cover and steel rails is 250 grams. $99.

Wilderness Trail Bikes SST-X. This is actually a unisex model, but it works for most women like it was made for them. As one tester commented, "While there's nothing remarkable—no cutouts, no cushions— it does what a good saddle should." It looks ordinary from the top, but from the side the company's distinctive down-turned nose is apparent. This allows you to move easily from sitting to standing and back without getting your shorts caught on the nose. The rounded rear helps you get off and on the back easily, too. The SST-X has just enough padding, and the dip between the nose and rear is positioned so a woman's soft parts don't get crushed. There are several models in the SST family of saddles, including ones with different padding thicknesses, rail materials, and Kevlar panels to protect the hips. Weight with leather cover and steel rails is 290 grams. $38.

Road Bike Seats

Avocet O2 Air 40W. This saddle looks like a T, having a broad rear that tapers to a narrow nose. The nose is 1½ inches shorter than the men's model and has a cutout to relieve pressure on soft genitalia. (The hole is covered, not visible.) This seat supports the theory that there's no saddle that will please every rider. One woman who tested it absolutely loved its cushioning and support, while another couldn't get comfortable at all. It's wider and softer than a typical racing saddle, making it a good choice for recreational or long-distance riders. Weight is 264 grams with a leather cover and titanium rails. $80. A version with steel rails and a synthetic cover costs $60.

Giro Fi'zi:k Vitesse. This is a stylin' saddle. All of our testers liked its sleek profile and split rear section. It sits high above the rails, which makes it easy to adjust, and the spotted suede cover enables shorts to "stick" so you don't slide unintentionally. The Vitesse has minimal padding. In fact, the only concession to the female form seems to be the wider rear. Serious road riders liked this saddle best, while casual cyclists found it uncomfortably firm. One tester said that its raised rear end gave her support that seemed to help her pedal more powerfully on climbs. Weight with titanium rails is 252 grams. $80.

Serfas Ladies Performance Dual Density. "Dual density" means that a hard plastic shell provides support while softer, flexible rubber inserts provide cushioning for the sit bones and genitalia. The women's model is shorter, wider, and a bit softer than the men's. Our testers thought that the broad rear enabled them to move back and climb better. One tester found the padding comfortable initially but too cushy on long rides. She sank into it so much that her crotch went numb. This seat is probably best for occasional riders. Weight with leather cover and titanium rails is 343 grams. $80. A version with steel rails costs $50.

Terry Pro Liberator. The Liberator has been around for years, but now it's also available in a lighter, narrower Pro version. Terry Precision Cycling for Women took a simple approach with the Liberator, cutting a hole in the nose of this saddle to relieve pressure. Our testers found it effective. The cutout eliminates contact and provides ventilation (particularly appreciated by those who've had to deal with yeast infections). Most felt that the padding was adequate and there was enough support for the sit bones. The only complaint: When you rotate forward to a low riding position, you can feel the edges of the hole. Some women find this uncomfortable. Weight is 254 grams with a leather cover and manganese rails. $60. The original Women's Liberator (slightly wider, shorter, and with steel rails) weighs 343 grams and costs $45.

Specialized Body Geometry. This unisex seat works for many women for the same reason that it helps men avoid genital numbness. The moderately padded top has a wedge-shaped cutout extending from the rear almost to the tip of the nose. This removes material where it would contact the crotch's soft tissues, but the sit bones remain fully supported. The nice thing is that you can't sense the edges of the wedge when riding, so this seat feels natural. Because the rear of the seat

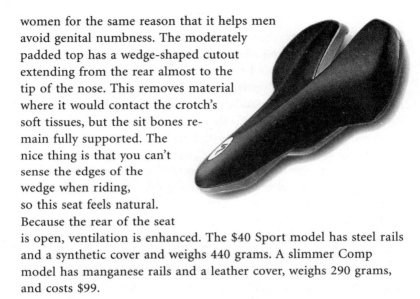

is open, ventilation is enhanced. The $40 Sport model has steel rails and a synthetic cover and weighs 440 grams. A slimmer Comp model has manganese rails and a leather cover, weighs 290 grams, and costs $99.

10
Clothes with Wheel Appeal

BY SUSAN WEAVER

If you're a new recruit to cycling, you may wonder why we dress the way we do. Comfort and ease of movement are the big motivators. Think about the sensitivity of the parts of your body that make contact with the bike—your hands, your feet, and your seat.

I'll save my breath and not talk about the bad ol' days when cycling clothing for women would fit only if you were built like a bicycle pump—or a man. Now it's easy to find clothing sized for our anatomy. But don't trust all makers who claim to make women-specific clothing. Check the garments themselves instead of just the labels. For instance, anomalies such as overly large armholes on sleeveless jerseys suggest that a manufacturer is merely offering women a downsized version of a men's cut instead of a gender-specific design.

Otherwise, it's all out there—fabric prints ranging from feminine to ferocious; a take-your-pick palette of pastels, brights, earth tones, and basic black. Garments cut for on-road, off-road, or casual pedaling. Styles that say cycling, and others that look more like traditional clothing. Here are some guidelines to help you shop.

Shorts, knickers, and tights. Putting thick-seamed shorts or blue jeans between you and the saddle will literally rub you the wrong way. You should wear cycling-specific shorts, tights, or knickers, which are designed to minimize bulk and prevent chafing.

The cling of spandex keeps shorts from riding up and exposing your thighs to chafing against the saddle. If you dislike the glossy racer look, you can find spandex blended with cotton or other materials. These reduce the shine but retain the form fit.

If the tight, second-skin look bothers you, go the camouflage route: made-for-cycling baggy shorts with built-in spandex shorts. These "baggies" have gained popularity for about-town cycling and trail use, although they're not going to be as comfortable as you'd like for long-distance road riding. And if you stand frequently as you ride, be forewarned that the outer shorts tend to catch on the nose of the saddle.

What's inside the garment counts, too. There should be a smooth, soft liner in the center that pads and protects you from friction. (This liner is often called a chamois, from the era when it was actually made of leather, but today's shorts use synthetic materials, which are more supple.) Check the liner to make sure it doesn't have a seam running through the center. This can irritate tender tissues. Most women prefer a construction with two curved seams ("baseball stitching") that keeps the center smooth. Even better is a molded, one-piece liner. Most shorts truly designed for women have one style or the other.

Under-the-liner padding may be fleece, gel, foam, or even liquid. Thicker may not mean better if the material bunches, so don't go by the amount of padding alone. Many liners have antibacterial treatment, which helps reduce the chance of developing saddle sores. By the way, lined cycling shorts are meant to be worn without underwear and washed after every use.

Don't ride in unlined garments. If you have multisport tights, wear cycling shorts under them or try a thigh-length padded brief made for the purpose.

Expect to pay from around $25 to $75 for a pair of cycling shorts. The same goes for long-legged cycling tights or knickers, which have legs that extend to just below the knee. The more expensive, the more individual panels (as many as eight) will be used in construction and, thus, the better the fit. Also, the liner and padding will be higher quality. A good pair of shorts, properly cared for, can easily last for several seasons.

Gloves. For road and off-road riding, several manufacturers offer gloves cut to fit women's narrower hands and wrists. Expect to pay $15 to $30. Most are lightly padded for comfort. Gloves protect your hands from all sorts of wear and tear and improve your grip on the handlebar, so think of them as a necessity rather than as an optional accessory.

Jerseys and crop tops. Cycling jerseys in women's proportions are available in more designs than ever. You can find virtually any cut, size, and neckline. Materials vary, but any good jersey will be made from a synthetic fabric that transports moisture away from your skin. Avoid cotton, which feels cold and clammy when damp.

Breezier crop tops come in short and to-the-waist lengths. The latter still provide air conditioning while reducing the wolf whistles. Some models have mesh panels for ventilation. Some come with built-in bras.

Whatever type of jersey you choose, it should have three rear pockets so you can easily carry snacks and other items. If you ride the road, choose colors that are bright enough to attract the eyes of motorists.

Jackets. A lightweight shell jacket that folds to slip into a jersey pocket or seatbag can save you from shivering if the air turns chilly or it begins to shower. Features to look for include zippered pockets for items that you want to keep handy, a front zipper that's easy to operate with one hand, comfortable elastic in the cuffs to keep sleeves where you want them, a tail long enough to cover you when you're bent toward the handlebar, and a color that makes you visible on a gray day. A shell should be made of breathable material or have vents so you don't create your own rain shower inside. One that's made of water-repellent illumi-NITE fabric has the added advantage of glowing in a vehicle's headlights—great insurance if you ever ride after dark.

Cover-ups. There may be times when you want to quickly put casual clothing over your cycling duds, like when you mix a ride with other activities and find yourself in a restaurant, store, party, or church, for example. I like to carry a cotton wrap-around skirt or a pair of sweatpants for such occasions. Some clothing companies make cover-ups that coordinate with their jerseys and shorts.

Shoes. Cycling shoes are necessary for serious riding because their rigid soles stop pedal pressure from hurting your feet. Shoes are designed for road riding or mountain biking, with the latter type offering the advantage of easier walking—the cleats for clipless pedals are recessed into the soles. Unfortunately, shoe selection is limited in the smallest women's sizes. You may have to try unisex sizing, which does accommodate many women.

Helmets. Good fit in a helmet means that it stays securely in place when you're riding over bumps and, most important, if you crash. To help this happen, many current helmets feature a "locking system" against the rear of the head. This extra strap customizes the fit and keeps the helmet from bouncing or moving too far forward or backward. With such a system, unisex helmets will probably fit most women. But ponytails can interfere with the locking system in some models, so if you tie back your hair for cycling, check before you buy. A few companies make helmets specifically for women, and ponytail clearance is not a problem with these.

PART THREE

Mechanical Matters

11
Fit for the Road

BY THE EDITORS OF *BICYCLING* MAGAZINE

Here's how to achieve a comfortable, efficient position on your road bike. By following these adjustment procedures and cycling techniques, you'll ride stronger and reduce your chance of sustaining aches and injuries to muscles or joints.

1. Neck. Try not to keep your head in one position for a long time. As you're riding, periodically tilt it or roll it to either side to reduce strain or stiffness.

2. Upper body/shoulders. Overall, let your legs do as much of the work as possible, not your upper body. Even when climbing or pedaling hard on the flats, keep your upper body and shoulders relaxed. Don't hunch them.

3. Arms. Keep your elbows slightly bent to absorb road shock, and hold them in line with your body, not splayed outward. Your arms will be more relaxed if your grip isn't overly tight.

4. Top-tube and stem length. Because women have relatively short torsos, extra attention must go into the top-tube and stem lengths when buying a bike. When you're sitting normally with your hands on the brake lever hoods and your arms slightly bent, the handlebar should obscure the front hub when you glance down. A new rider should aim for a straight back positioned at about a 50-degree angle to the ground. With flexibility and experience, you should evolve into a 45-degree position and possibly need a stem that's 1 or 2 cm longer. This will aid aerodynamics, improve pedaling power, and help straighten your back.

5. Stem height. The top of the handlebar stem should be about an inch below the top of the saddle. If you can lower it a little farther without upper-body or breathing discomfort, do so. It will make you more aerodynamic.

6. Handlebar. The bottom, flat portions of the handlebar (known as the drops) should be level or angled slightly down toward the rear brake. Handlebar width should equal shoulder width. This opens your chest to facilitate breathing without creating unnecessary wind drag.

7. Brake levers. Wrists should be straight when you're grasping the levers with your hands in the hooks of a drop handlebar. To accomplish this, set the levers' positions so their tips just touch a straightedge extended from the bottoms of the drops.

8. Hands. Don't hold the handlebar in a death grip. Place your hands down in the hooks or on the drops when going fast or riding into a headwind. Grasp the brake lever hoods on top for easy-paced, flatland riding. Sit up and hold the top of the bar for added leverage and easier breathing on long, steady climbs. Change hand position often to avoid the constant pressure that can make hands become numb. When standing, grasp the hoods lightly and gently rock the bike from side to side in synch with your pedal strokes. Always keep your thumb and at least one finger closed around the hood or bar to prevent losing your grip on bumps.

9. Back. Whether riding on the brake hoods or the drops, your back should be straight, not bowed or hunched. If you rotate the top of your hips forward, you will minimize the bend in your lower back. It helps to imagine that you're trying to point your belly button at the top tube.

10. Butt. During normal riding, your sit bones should be perched on the broader rear portion of the seat. If it isn't wide enough in the rear

for proper support (or if you are uncomfortable in this position), re-place the saddle with a model that's anatomically designed for women. For better leverage, slide backward on the saddle when climbing or pushing big gears. Move forward for increased leg speed during sprints or other short, hard efforts.

11. Saddle height. The distance measured from the center of the crankset axle, along the seat tube, to the top of the saddle should be 0.883 of your inseam length (measured in stocking feet from floor to crotch). When height is right, your knees will be slightly bent at the bottom of the pedal stroke, and, when viewed from behind, your hips will not rock as you pedal. Raise the saddle an extra 2 to 3 mm if you have large feet for your height. If your present saddle height is way off, make changes 2 mm at a time over the course of several rides in order to avoid knee or muscle strain.

12. Saddle tilt. The saddle should be level or pointed very slightly down at the nose, depending on what feels better. Don't tilt the nose down any more than it takes to relieve pressure or you will slide for-ward, putting additional weight on your arms and knees.

13. Knee-over-pedal. A weighted string held to the front of your for-ward knee should touch the end of the crankarm when you're seated comfortably with the crankarms horizontal. Adjust as necessary by sliding the saddle fore or aft. Or you may wish to try a slight variation. Placing your saddle 1 to 2 cm farther back fosters a more powerful ped-aling style for climbing or time trialing. Moving it 1 to 2 cm forward aids spinning and sprinting.

14. Frame. Frame size should result in 4 to 5 inches of exposed seat-post once saddle height is correct. (Frame size refers to seat-tube length, generally measured from the center of the crankset axle to the top of the top tube.) Overall, a smaller frame is desirable for lightness and stiff-ness. However, don't use such a small frame that the top tube is too short or the seatpost must be raised past the maximum-extension line engraved near its end.

15. Feet. To prevent knee injury, shoe cleats should be adjusted so that the angle of your feet on the pedals is natural. Think of your foot-prints when you walk from a swimming pool—some people's feet angle outward, while others' are pigeon-toed. The Rotational Adjustment De-vice (RAD), part of the Fit Kit bicycle sizing system used by many shops, can help transfer your natural foot position to the bike. Or you can reduce the need for precision by using a pedal system that allows your feet to freely pivot ("float") several degrees and find their natural angle. Either way, cleat placement should put the widest part of each foot directly above or slightly in front of the pedal axle. If you use toe-clips, be sure they allow about ¼ inch of clearance beyond the tips of your shoes. If the clips are too close, you'll have a hard time getting your feet in and out. Put washers between the clips and pedals or install the next larger size.

16. Pedaling technique. You need a clipless pedal system or toeclips with straps for optimum pedaling efficiency. Concentrate on feeling the pedal all the way around and making smooth circles. Use your hamstrings to pull back at the bottom of each stroke (a motion similar to that used to scrape mud off the bottom of your foot), then raise your heel on the upstroke and bring your knee forward toward the handlebar. This helps eliminate dead spots, where no force is being applied.

17. Crankarm length. In general, if your inseam is less than 29 inches, use 165-mm crankarms; 29 to 32 inches, 170-mm; 33 to 34 inches, 172.5-mm; and more than 34 inches, 175-mm. Crankarm length is measured from the center of the crankarm axle bolt to the center of the pedal hole. But you won't need a ruler—the length is engraved on the back.

12
Fit for the Trails

BY THE EDITORS OF *BICYCLING* MAGAZINE

It's important to have a comfortable, efficient position on your mountain bike. By following these adjustment procedures and cycling techniques, you'll handle the varied terrain and conditions that make mountain biking so thrilling, and you'll reduce your chance of sustaining aches and injuries to muscles or joints.

1. Upper body. Strive for a loose, relaxed upper body.

2. Arms. For shock absorption and steering control, your elbows should be comfortably bent, even when you slide well back on the saddle. If you can reach the handlebar only with your elbows locked, get a shorter stem, look for a frame with a shorter top tube, or learn to lean forward more. If your upper arms and shoulders fatigue quickly because you are too cramped, you may need a longer stem or a frame with a longer top tube.

3. Top-tube and stem length. These combine to govern handlebar reach, an aspect of fit to which women should pay particular attention. With a mountain bike's extra-long seatpost, it's often top-tube length, not seat-tube length, that dictates whether to buy a smaller or larger frame size (or even a different make of bicycle). The result should be slightly bent arms and a straight back.

4. Stem height and rise angle. These should place the handlebar 1 to 3 inches below the top of the saddle if you intend to ride trails. This shifts enough weight to the front wheel for climbing control. If you need a high-rise stem, get one. Don't raise a too-low stem past its maximum-extension line—it could snap off or pull out. If your bike has a threadless headset, minimal or no stem-height adjustment can be made; alterations depend on the rise angle.

5. Handlebar. Bar width should feel comfortable and natural with your hands on the grips—21 to 24 inches is common on mountain bikes. Since women's shoulders are normally narrower than men's, many women are likely to find narrower handlebars comfortable yet wide enough for good slow-speed control. (In general, the narrower the bar, the quicker the steering.) If necessary, you can shorten the ends with a hacksaw or pipe cutter. First, though, move your controls and grips inward and take a ride to make sure you'll like the new width. If it's too narrow, you won't be able to control the steering sufficiently. Leave a bit extra at each end if you use (or want to add) bar-ends.

Bars come with varying degrees of rearward sweep, from 0 to about 12 degrees. (A few have as much as 22 degrees.) Try them to see which gives the most natural wrist position. Note that changing the rearward sweep also alters the reach to the grips and could require a different stem extension.

6. Hands and wrists. Try to ride as relaxed as possible without sacrificing a firm grip. Usually, holding the handlebar with pinkie and ring fingers is sufficient, leaving the index and middle fingers to operate the brakes. Keep your thumbs wrapped under the grips, not on top where a jolt could cause your hands to slip off. On rough terrain, grasp the bar firmly to transfer shock to your arms (keeping your elbows bent). A light grip lets the bar vibrate against your hands, causing stinging or numbness. Although squishy foam grips feel good on the showroom floor, firmer, less compressible ones fatigue your hands less and give you a better sense of the terrain under the wheels.

7. Back. A forward lean of at least 45 degrees is most efficient because the strong gluteus muscles of the butt aren't able to contribute as much pedaling power when you're sitting more upright. This forward lean also shifts weight to your arms, so your butt doesn't get as sore. New riders, don't be impatient with yourselves if you can't lean that far forward at first; you'll develop flexibility over time.

8. Butt. When riding, don't always sit squarely in the middle of the saddle. Slide to the rear for added power or to keep the back wheel planted on descents (on steep or bumpier descents, you'll even learn to push your butt off the back of the saddle). On steep climbs, crouching over the handlebar while sitting on the saddle nose maintains traction and keeps the front wheel down.

9. Saddle height. The distance from the center of the crankset axle to the top of the saddle should be 0.883 of your inseam length (measured in stocking feet from floor to crotch). Your knees should be slightly bent

at the bottom of the pedal stroke, and, when viewed from behind, your hips should not rock as you pedal. For descents, on a bike so-equipped, a beginner can use the seatpost quick-release to lower the saddle an inch or so to lower the center of gravity; raise the saddle once you're on the level again.

10. Saddle tilt. Most female riders prefer level saddles, but some like a slight nose-down tilt to avoid irritation. A nose-up position can put painful pressure on the genitals when you're leaning forward.

11. Seatpost. On a properly fitted mountain bike, you'll see more seatpost showing than you would on a road bike. That's why off-road posts are commonly 300 to 350 mm long. Don't raise the post above the maximum-extension line that's engraved on it.

12. Knee-over-pedal. Don't use fore/aft saddle position to compensate for improper handlebar reach—that's why stems come in different lengths. When you're seated comfortably, a plumb line dropped from the front of the forward kneecap should touch the end of the crankarm when it's horizontal. Slide the saddle forward or back to achieve this.

13. Frame. You need a lot of crotch clearance so you don't hurt yourself if you need to hop off. This isn't as critical for pavement and smooth dirt riding. There's no advantage, however, to riding a frame any larger than the smallest size that provides enough seat height. Smaller frames are lighter, shorter, and more maneuverable.

Beware—the numbers can be confusing: Some manufacturers measure frame size from the center of the bottom bracket to the center of the top tube, others to the top of the top tube, and others to the top of an extended seat lug. Plus, mountain bikes have sloping top tubes that result in relatively short seat tubes. In this situation, a 13- or 14-inch mountain bike could be the ideal size for someone who rides a 19-inch road bike. The safest way to determine if a frame fits is to road-test it before buying.

14. Feet. If you use toeclips, there should be at least 5 mm (almost ¼ inch) of clearance between the tip of your shoe and the front of the clip when the ball of your foot is over the pedal axle. Because mountain bike shoes are bulky, toeclips for off-road use run larger than road bike clips.

15. Pedaling technique. Smoothness is desirable. However, a mountain bike's longer crankarms, combined with riding steeper climbs and rough terrain, contribute to a slower cadence. On rough trails, pushing a higher gear at a lower cadence lets your legs bear most of your weight, lessening shock to your arms and butt. Ride really bumpy terrain out of the saddle in the "ready position," crouched over the bike so it's free to chatter and bounce under you.

16. Crankarm length. This usually varies with frame size. For added climbing leverage, the same size rider usually uses 5-mm larger crankarms on a mountain bike than on a road bike. In general, most mountain bikes come with 175-mm crankarms, and in most cases these work fine. Upgrading to an unusual length (such as 177.5 or 180) can be expensive, so only do this if you're sure the stock length is causing problems. If so, use inseam measurement to select crankarm length. If your inseam is less than 29 inches, use 170-mm crankarms; 29 to 32 inches, 175-mm; 33 to 34 inches, 177.5-mm; and more than 34 inches, 180-mm. (Crankarms are measured from the center of the crankarm axle bolt to the center of the pedal mounting hole; the size is usually marked on the back.)

13
You, the Bike Mechanic

BY CARLOTTA CUERDON

I'm an enthusiastic cyclist. Road, dirt, track—I've been doing it all for years. But my enthusiasm is for actually riding the bike, not cleaning it, not sitting around discussing the finer points of its design, and certainly not repairing it.

I tried to pay attention when people showed me how to repair a flat, fix my chain, or even how the roof rack works. But somehow the information never stayed in my head, and I'd feel like the kid sister when I had a breakdown and someone else had to make the repair. But they loved me at the local bike shop.

And then I got lucky. I married a guy who fixed bikes in a shop for 4 years and went on to write many articles on bike repair. My husband would fix my bike before I even knew there was a problem.

In contrast, my friend Liz had no one but herself to maintain her bike. I had long considered myself more of an expert on bikes than her (simply because I started riding first). Then I caught her adjusting her rear derailleur and discussing the merits of her Kevlar-belted tires with my husband and realized that she may be the lucky one.

Inspired by Liz's example and reminded of the dangers of breaking down by myself on a lonely road or trail, I prevailed upon my husband for yet another repair lesson. I listened patiently and tried my hand at a few things, but it was no use. Fifteen minutes was all it took before I was stifling yawns. Learning to fix my bike was boring.

So although I had been shown how to fix a flat, read about the procedure (complete with pictures), and even done a few of the steps—in the safety of the kitchen—I had never actually changed a tire from start to finish under combat conditions. You know what I mean—by the side of the road, miles from anywhere, cars whizzing by, and maybe the sun setting to heighten the urgency.

But I got my chance, like all cyclists will sooner or later. One bright spring morning, I was riding with my mom when she flatted. I rode 3 miles back to the bike shop to see if my husband would help us. (See how far I would go to avoid a repair?) But he was away on an errand.

Well, this was it. Fix it or walk. And so, working together, combining our limited experience and passing the wheel back and forth when the going got tough, my mom and I changed the tube. After the last bit of air was pumped in and we saw that it actually stayed in, we whooped with joy. Our fingers were sore, we had smudges on our arms and legs, and we hadn't broken any speed records. But it taught me one simple thing that's enabled me to tighten seat bolts, align brake pads, and adjust derailleurs: If you gotta do it, you'll find it in yourself.

So, all you bike-repair neophytes, take it from one who's been there. If you're not the kind who learns from a demonstration, you'll learn from hands-on experience. All you need is the opportunity—and you'll surely get it. One day, you'll be out on your own and a tire will lose air or something will break. Get ready by reading the next two chapters and giving bike repair a try. If you have a knack for it, get a copy of *Bicycling Magazine's Basic Maintenance and Repair* (another book in this series), and there will be virtually nothing on your bike that you won't be able to fix. But even if you feel all of the techno-whiz blowing right by you, don't worry. Just by trying, you'll be learning more than you think; and when you need to make an adjustment or minor repair to get home safely, chances are, you'll do okay.

P.S.—Just remember to pack a spare tube, a patch kit, and some tools, primarily a pump, tire levers, and a multitool that contains a chain tool, allen wrenches, and screwdrivers.

14
It's Easy to Fix a Flat

BY JIM LANGLEY

Sooner or later, it will happen. You'll be pedaling merrily along when you hear hissing or a sudden kapow, and one end of the bike will sink. Yep, it's a flat tire, by far the most common breakdown you'll face as a cyclist. Worry not. The repair is simple.

To guarantee that you'll laugh away your next flat, here's a step-by-step tube-replacement guide. Make a copy to keep in your seatbag with your repair kit. You won't need instructions after you've done the procedure a few times.

I'll assume that you've flatted while riding. If you're working at home and have access to a floor pump and a repair stand, by all means use them. On the road, it's not necessary to support the bike, but you may be able to by hooking the nose of the saddle over a fence or low branch. Or ask a riding partner to hold the bike while you operate.

1. Open the brake. To make it easy to remove the wheel and put it back in, most brakes can be widened. For a cantilever brake, squeeze both brake pads against the rim with one hand and unhook the transverse cable from the brake arm (see photo). That's the short cable that passes over the wheel to join the two arms. For sidepulls, look for a small lever on the caliper or brake lever and open it to spread the pads (see photo). For parallel-pull brakes (such as the Shimano V-Brakes found on many mountain bikes), squeeze the pads against the rim with one hand and pull the noodle (the L-shaped piece of tubing that the cable passes through) out of its holder in the brake arm, which will allow the brake to open.

2. Remove the wheel. Most bikes have quick-release (QR) hubs so wheels can be removed without tools. If it's a rear flat, first hand-shift onto the smallest cog to move the derailleur fully to the outside. Next, open the QR by flipping the lever 180 degrees. You should feel it loosen,

and you may see the word "open" on the lever. It helps to pull the derailleur back with one hand as you push the wheel forward and down with the other (see photo). That's all it takes to remove the wheel. Then, support the bike on something or lay it on its left side so the drivetrain won't be against the ground (you don't want sand in your chain). Front wheels won't necessarily come off when the QR is

opened. Many bikes have nubs on the fork dropouts that capture the QR to prevent the wheel from dislodging if the lever is improperly tightened. If this is your setup, hold either end of the QR and unscrew the other until it clears the nubs. Then remove the wheel.

3. Remove the old tube. If any air remains, deflate the tube completely. Depress a Schrader valve (which resembles a car-tire valve) with the corner of a tire lever; unscrew and depress the top of a presta valve. Then hold the wheel upright and slide a tire lever under one edge of the tire (the "bead") on the opposite side of the wheel from

the valve stem. Pull the lever down to pry the bead over the rim, and hold the lever or hook it to a spoke. Place the second lever under the same bead, about 4 inches from the first lever, and pull it down, too (see photo). Repeat the process, leapfrogging the levers. Soon, a section of the bead will be off, and you should be able to slide a lever around the rim to free that entire side of the tire. Then reach inside and extract the tube.

Note: A presta valve may be held through the rim by a nut or knurled ring, which must be unscrewed before the tube can be removed.

4. Install a new tube. The easiest way to fix a flat during a ride is to replace the tube. Save the punctured one to patch at home, then make it

your spare. Before installing a fresh tube, you must check the tire to see if whatever caused the flat is still sticking through. Gingerly feel all the way around the inside circumference. If you have a rag, wad it and slide it in both directions (see photo). It will catch on anything sharp. If you find something, carefully pick it out with a fingernail or poke it out with your minitool. Next, inflate the fresh tube just enough to unflatten it and remove any wrinkles. Put the valve stem through the hole, then feed the tube into the tire. If necessary, let some air out so the tube fits without folds.

5. Attach the tire. Start at the valve stem and work with both hands in each direction to push the loose edge of the tire over the rim. You'll wind up on the side opposite the stem with several inches still to go. This last section can be tough to get on, especially for skinny road-bike tires. If you have a problem, go back to the stem and fully deflate the tube. Also, wiggle

Handy Helper

The hardest part of replacing a tube can be getting those final few inches of tire back onto the rim. If you find yourself struggling with this part of the procedure, check out a nifty product called the Crank Brothers Speed Lever. It snaps onto the hub axle and telescopes to reach the rim. You hook it under the tire and simply slide it to lift the bead over the rim. There's no danger of pinching and puncturing the new tube.

This device also works in reverse, helping you remove the tire. The Speed Lever sells in bike shops for less than $10.

the valve stem and push it up into the tire to make sure the tube isn't caught under the beads. Pinch the two beads of the tire together so they fit into the deep center portion of the rim, and continue doing this as you work your way around to the obstinate section. Place the wheel on your knee, hold one end of the uninstalled section to keep it in place, then use your thumbs or the heel of your stronger hand to roll the bead up and over (see photo). Resist using tire levers, because there's danger of pinching a hole in the tube. After the tire is mounted, go back to the valve stem and push it up into the tire again to make sure the tube isn't caught under the beads, then pull it down.

6. Inflate the tire. Place the pump on the valve. Grasp the head and brace it by wrapping your thumb over the tire and your finger behind a spoke so you won't bend or break the valve stem when pumping force-fully (see photo). Inflate to half-

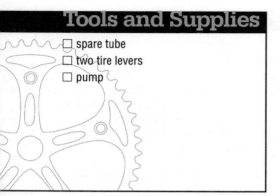

Tools and Supplies

- ☐ spare tube
- ☐ two tire levers
- ☐ pump

pressure, then check for proper seating. A fine line molded into the tire sidewall (called the bead line) should appear just above the rim and be equidistant from it all the way around on both sides. Spin the wheel to eye this. If the line bows above the rim, it means the tube is caught under the bead and will blow out if you keep pumping. Deflate the tire and wiggle this section to get the tube inside the tire. Sometimes you may have to carefully poke the tube with a tire lever. If the bead line dips below the rim, keep pumping and it should pop up.

7. Install the wheel. For a front wheel, stand the bike up and center the wheel in the fork with the quick-release (QR) lever on the bike's left side. Make sure the wheel's axle is fully inserted in the dropouts. If you had to unscrew the QR to bypass dropout nubs, hold the lever open and turn the nut clockwise. The adjustment is correct when the QR begins to clamp after you've closed the lever about halfway (see photo). The force required to finish should be enough to leave an impression on your palm, and the lever should wind up tucked next to the fork blade. The procedure is similar for the rear wheel, but clamping the QR should be as easy as flipping the lever because you didn't need to change its adjustment. When in-

stalling a rear wheel, remember to set the chain on the smallest cog, where it was when you removed the wheel. Make sure the tire is centered between the chainstays behind the bottom bracket and the seatstays by the brake. Close the QR so that the lever ends up between the left chainstay and seatstay, where it can't be loosened accidentally. Finish the job by hooking up the brake cable or by closing the brake QR.

15

Simple Bike Care Tips

BY JIM LANGLEY

Apart from the few minutes required, no great effort or mechanical expertise is needed to keep a bike in great shape. And there are big pay-offs. A well-maintained bike rides better and is safer and more reliable. It will last longer and then have greater resale value. When you learn how your bike works and how to keep it adjusted, you ride with greater confidence. If there should be a problem during a ride, you'll probably know how to make an emergency repair.

All of these benefits arise from simply attending to your bike's mechanical needs about once a week or month (depending on how frequently you ride and the weather conditions). It will still need a professional overhaul occasionally—every bike does—but the shop mechanics will love working on your clean machine. And your bill may be less because it saves them time.

Sold? Okay, here are eight home-maintenance recommendations designed to keep your bike running as good as new.

1. Store it. Parking your bike inside is the easiest way to keep it working and looking like new. Nothing is worse for a bike than constant exposure to the elements. In coastal areas, the air is so caustic that it will actually eat the metal and rubber. If you're strapped for room, buy a plastic-coated bike hook at any shop and screw it into a ceiling

Tools and Supplies

- [ ] floor pump with gauge
- [ ] minipump
- [ ] bucket
- [ ] detergent
- [ ] sponges
- [ ] brushes
- [ ] biodegradable solvent
- [ ] rags
- [ ] emery cloth
- [ ] awl
- [ ] drip or spray lubricant
- [ ] bike wax
- [ ] 12-inch ruler
- [ ] assorted small wrenches

stud in a corner. Then the bike can hang vertically. Or you can suspend it upside down by the wheels from two hooks in the ceiling. Be creative, or even decorative. Maybe there's enough space in a closet, over a stairwell, or over your bed. If you can't put hooks in your ceiling or walls, consider a free-standing rack that will hold your bike up and out of the way.

2. Inflate it. Most tubes are made of butyl rubber, a porous material that allows gradual loss of air. If you ride on soft tires, you risk damage

to both them and the rims should you hit a pothole or rock. Mushy tires also make it harder to pedal. Buy a floor pump with a built-in gauge and check tire pressure at least once per week. Keep it in the recommended range that's listed on the tire sidewall or label (see photo). In addition, buy a pump to carry on your bike. You'll need it to fix a flat or keep you rolling on a slow leak until you get home.

3. Clean it. All it takes is dishwashing detergent, warm water, and a couple of sponges and brushes. Wash the entire bike from top to bottom, including the tires and rims. If the chain is grimy, clean it by brushing it with a biodegradable solvent, wiping it with a rag, then washing it with soap and water. Rinse the bike with a hose or pail of clean water, but don't direct it at the headset, bottom bracket, hubs, or pedals, because water can enter their bearings and break down the grease. If you can't get the braking surfaces on the rim sidewalls completely clean, lightly sand them with emery cloth. Look at the faces of the brake pads, too, and pick out any pebbles or deposits with an awl so that they can't gouge the rims.

4. Lube it. A bike will corrode and work poorly if not lubricated. After washing and drying, use a bike-specific drip or spray lube on the chain, derailleur and brake pivots, and places where cables enter or exit housings. Wipe off any overspray or excess. If the cable stops on your frame are slotted, you can also lube the gear and brake cables. Do this to the former by shifting onto the largest cog, then moving the lever back to its starting position without pedaling. This creates cable slack, allowing you to pull the housing from the cable stops and slide it to expose and lube the hidden sections (see photo). For brakes, open the quick-release to create cable slack, then follow the same procedure. To minimize dirt's adherence to the frame, use a bike-specific wax. Unlike most

car waxes, it won't cause a chalky buildup in tight areas.

5. Inspect it. A bike lasts longest if you keep an eye on the components and replace things before they become too worn. Start with the frame. Look for rippled paint or bulges near the tube intersections. These are signs of damage or impending failure, usually caused by rough treatment. Such signs should be checked professionally. Check the tire treads and brake pads for wear. If pads are worn to the point that their grooves are gone, replace them. Check the handlebar tape or grips for slipping, cracking, or peeling. Study the cable housing for damage where it enters the brakes, derailleurs, levers, and guides on the frame. Squeeze and hold the brake levers to see if the cables are rusted or frayed anywhere along their run. Measure the chain. A new one is exactly 12 inches from the center of any pin to the center of another. If the second pin exceeds the 12-inch mark by 1/8 inch or more, the chain is worn and should be replaced.

6. Tighten it. Components may loosen with use, which can lead to premature wear or even an accident. Every month, check the tightness of the pedals (the left one has backward threads, so it tightens counterclockwise), crankarm bolts, chainring bolts, stem and handlebar binder bolts, seat and seatpost binder bolts, suspension bolts, derailleur and brake-cable anchor bolts, and accessory mounting bolts. If a bolt is snug, stop. Overtightening a bike's small bolts can cause them to strip or break.

7. Adjust it. Most bikes rely on cable-operated brakes and gears. In time, these cables stretch, reducing responsiveness and precision. Fortunately, most brake and derailleur systems have barrel adjusters so you can

(continued on page 60)

A Woman's Guide to Front Suspension

Most suspension forks on mountain bikes come from the factory adjusted for a 150- to 170-pound rider, which means that anyone weighing less than that should change the setup. If you don't, the fork won't soak up bumps well enough to give you the benefits of greater comfort and control.

Also, women have special needs thanks to our anatomy. Because we carry more of our weight in our hips, we have less weight over a bike's front end than do men of the same size. This is compounded by the short, high-rise stems many women prefer. These further unweight the bike's front end and make it more difficult to initiate the fork's movement. Our generally less aggressive riding style also dictates that we adjust our forks differently—for little and medium bumps rather than big hits.

A good solution if you're shopping for a mountain bike is to get one that has an elastomer fork. This type is quick and supple—best for lighter riders because it suffers less "stiction" (static friction) than hydraulic (air/oil) forks. In other words, an elastomer fork moves more readily. In addition, it can easily be tuned—adjusted for your weight. Fortunately, the forks that are found most often on mountain bikes in the low- and mid-price ranges are elastomer models. These forks can be tuned by changing the elastomers or adjusting preload.

CHANGE ELASTOMERS

Crudely put, elastomers are rubber bumpers that compress to absorb impacts. Often, there are several stacked like doughnuts in each fork leg. They come in different hardnesses ("durometers"). Most manufacturers use a color code.

"I recommend that you go as light as possible," says Jamie Griffis, a mechanic and founder of a women's mountain biking club in California. "From the get-go, put in the softest bumpers. A woman should do that before she even leaves the shop with her new bike." Fork makers Rock Shox and Answer produce soft-ride kits with replacement elastomers, priced between $20 and $35.

Changing elastomers is easy. At the top of each fork leg is one knob. For example, on the Answer Manitou Mach 5 SX, the knobs adjust preload, which is the adjustable spring tension in a suspension fork or rear suspension. It determines how far the suspension compresses under body weight and how much travel remains to absorb impacts. The knobs sit on top caps, which are what you need to unscrew. Turn each top cap fully counterclockwise (with Channel-lock pliers if necessary, after protecting the cap with a rag) and pull out the attached elastomers. The Manitou Mach 5 Comp has only a single long one. Remove it (you may have to turn the bike upside-down) and replace it with a soft blue one. The SX and the Manitou Mach 5 Pro have a stack of three elastomers on a skewer. Remove them, lightly grease the skewer, and replace them with softer ones.

ADJUST PRELOAD

After you install the softer elastomers, adjust preload to fine-tune your fork. Less preload means easier fork movement. "Start at the easiest setting and work your way harder, if you need to," advises Robin Stuart, author of *Mountain Biking for Women* and a mountain biking instructor.

For example, there's a knob atop Rock Shox fork legs in some models. Unscrew it fully counterclockwise to decrease preload. It's that simple. Older Rock Shox Quadra models have a black plastic plug at the top of each fork leg instead of a knob. Pull out the plug using your fingernail. Underneath is a 4-mm allen bolt set inside an 8-mm allen bolt. Use a 4-mm allen wrench to adjust preload and an 8-mm allen wrench to unscrew the top cap for elastomer replacement.

The Manitou Mach 5 SX has a preload knob like that of the Rock Shox. Simply unscrew it fully counterclockwise. Other Answer forks require that you remove the top caps to make preload adjustments. At the base of each cap are five grooves. A C-shaped metal ring ("circlip") sits in the middle groove. To lessen preload, remove the circlip and slide it into one of the lower grooves.

How do you know when you have your fork set up correctly? Most elastomer models should have at least 2 inches of travel. To check this, push the protective rubber boot up to the top of the fork leg. Place a zip-tie snugly around the bottom of the exposed stanchion tube. Cut off any excess, then pull the boot back down over the zip-tie. Go for a ride, making sure to include some serious bumps. When the fork compresses, the tie will be pushed up the stanchion and stay there. Afterward, carefully peel the boot up and measure how far the tie has moved. This indicates maximum travel. If it doesn't approach 2 inches, soften your fork some more. On the other hand, if the fork moves too readily and you feel it bottom out with a harsh thunk on big bumps, it's too soft.

If your fork brand and model isn't mentioned here, don't fret. The tuning procedure is probably similar. For specifics, read the owner's manual supplied by your bike's fork manufacturer. If you don't have it, check with a shop that sells your brand or check the Internet, as many companies have sites devoted to their products.

By Delaine Fragnoli

retension cables without tools. You can find these barrels where the cables enter the component or the lever. Simply turn the barrels counterclockwise to remove slack. On a rear derailleur, the barrel is found where the cable enters at the rear (see photo). Adjust in half-turn increments until shifts are quick and quiet again. A front derailleur may not have a barrel. For brakes, turn the bar-

rels to compensate for cable stretch or pad wear, or to get the lever action that you like. The barrels on most mountain bike levers have separate lockrings that you can screw down to retain the adjustment.

8. Baby it. Like all machines, a bicycle will work best and last a long time if it's used with some respect. Sure, a mountain bike is built for hard riding, but this doesn't mean it's okay to thrash it. With practice, you'll learn to "ride light," getting off the saddle in rough terrain to let your knees and elbows absorb the beating that otherwise would be concentrated on the wheels and frame. When it's necessary to jump obstacles, make the landing soft by again absorbing the blow with bent legs and arms. Don't run head on into curbs, logs, or rocks until you develop the ability to lift the front wheel first, then shift your weight forward to lighten rear impact. Make gear changes only when you have light or moderate pressure on the pedals, thereby reducing the chance of drivetrain damage or excessive wear. Prevent skids so you save the wheels and tires (as well as the environment when riding off-road). And try to avoid crashing. It's not only hard on your body, it's tough on your wheels and frame.

PART FOUR

Body Talk

16

Cycling during Your Cycle

BY JULIE WALSH

A woman's monthly reproductive cycle doesn't just affect fertility. It influences mood, muscle mass, body-fat percentage, energy, metabolism, and aerobic capacity—all important factors for cycling.

World championships have been won by women during all phases of their menstrual cycles, yet many women complain of feeling tired, heavy, uncomfortable, clumsy, or weak during certain times of the month, especially just before and at the beginning of menstruation. Here's a look at what medical research and experts have to say about this complex issue, plus some tips on how to ride your best even on bad-hormone days. But first, let's see what happens in the normal menstrual cycle.

The Regular Cycle

There are two main phases of the menstrual cycle. They're separated by ovulation, the release of a mature egg into the fallopian tubes. The number of days from the first day of your period to ovulation is called the follicular phase. (It's usually 11 to 14 days.) The days after ovulation until the first day of your next period is called the luteal phase (also usually 11 to 14 days). During the follicular phase, levels of the two main sex hormones, estrogen and progesterone, are low. Around ovulation, estrogen peaks while progesterone remains low. During the luteal phase, both hormones are at high levels. The luteal phase is when many metabolic changes occur that can alter performance—for better and, possibly, for worse.

"During the luteal phase, high levels of estrogen and progesterone may facilitate more carbohydrate storage in your muscles and liver, and your metabolism shifts to burn more free fatty acids as fuel. Theoretically, for endurance cyclists, this could be a major benefit," explains Connie Lebrun, M.D., director of primary-care sports medicine at the Fowler-Kennedy Sport Medicine Clinic at the University of Western Ontario.

But research on the topic hasn't yet produced conclusive results.

Some studies show improved athletic performance during the luteal phase, while others show no benefit. And surveys of female athletes reveal nothing except great individual variations.

In one of the best studies to date, Dr. Lebrun measured max VO$_2$ (the maximum amount of oxygen that can be consumed during all-out exertion), anaerobic capacity, high-intensity endurance and strength, and body weight and fat of 16 athletic women during both phases of their menstrual cycles. The results revealed a slight decline of max VO$_2$ in the luteal phase, but the decline was only of marginal statistical significance, says Dr. Lebrun. "For most women, their cycles probably won't affect performance. But for a small percentage of athletes, these cyclical changes in max VO$_2$ may be significant enough to alter performance."

Take Control

For now, there's no bottom line. But that doesn't mean you should let your hormones rule and stay off the saddle, sitting on your duff and feeding your fat or sugar cravings. Here are several things you can do to ride your best, no matter how bad a hormone day you're having.

Stay active. "One of the best things you can do to combat hormonal fluctuations is to get regular physical activity," says Suzanne Tanner, M.D., sports medicine physician at the University of Colorado Health Science Center in Denver. Research shows that exercise helps decrease the severity of physical changes during the menstrual cycle, and it definitely improves mood.

Log your menstrual cycle. Use a training log and add how you're feeling—physically and emotionally—along with where you are in your menstrual cycle. After a few months, review the data to see if there's a correlation between performance and cycle phase. This data can help you schedule important rides or races during the best days of the month. If you use birth control pills, you can work with your doctor to alter your cycle to be at your best for an important ride. (If you do this, however, you can't rely on the Pill for birth control during that month.)

Change your diet. Some research indicates that you can alleviate many PMS symptoms by watching what you eat. You should increase carbohydrate and fluid intake but eat less fat and protein. Also, avoid alcohol, caffeine, and excessively salty foods.

Consider the Pill. Although no drug is without side effects, the newer, low-dose estrogen and progesterone birth control pills have fewer (weight gain, lowered max VO$_2$) than in the past, notes Dr. Tanner. And the Pill has many advantages. "Taking a birth control pill keeps your hormones on a more even keel throughout the month," she says. It also makes your periods regular and predictable so you can plan for them. In addition, the flow is light (a major plus for long rides), and premenstrual symptoms are often minimized. The estrogen may also have other performance and health benefits, such as allowing your body to store more glycogen and reducing the risk of certain cancers. Consult your obstetrician/gynecologist to see if the Pill is appropriate for you.

17
Riding while Pregnant

BY SARA J. HENRY

You love to ride, you're pregnant, and you're worried (quite understandably) about hurting that junior cyclist-to-be. What's a mom to do? Start by getting answers to the key concerns of every expectant mother on wheels.

Can I keep riding? Generally, the answer is simple: yes. You should discuss it with your doctor, but chances are that you'll get plenty of encouragement. Exercise helps keep you from gaining too much weight while it keeps you healthy and happy.

If, however, you fall into a risk category—say, you are carrying more than one child or have high blood pressure, diabetes, or some other complication—your doctor may give you specific exercise guidelines. Some high-risk women will be advised against exercising at all.

How long and hard can I ride? It depends on how you feel. Although older guidelines from the American College of Obstetrics and Gynecology (ACOG) recommended that you keep your heart rate under 140 beats per minute, the current guidelines recognize that an absolute of this kind isn't practical for everyone. Now ACOG advises clearing all exercise with your doctor, avoiding exhaustion, and stopping when you're tired. ACOG also points out that exercising regularly—at least three times per week—is better than sporadic training.

The Melpomene Institute in St. Paul, Minnesota, which studies physical activity and women's health, suggests avoiding a breathless pace. Susan Cushman, M.D., an obstetrician and Melpomene cofounder, recommends exercising at two-thirds of your normal intensity. Pregnancy is no time to prove your toughness.

How do I know if I'm overdoing it? If you're a seasoned rider, you're probably used to ignoring minor discomforts. But that needs to change when you're pregnant. "You don't want to blow off pain that in the past you would simply work through," says James Byrne, M.D., an obstetrician/gynecologist in maternal fetal medicine at the University of Southern California in Los Angeles. Your heart and lungs are already working harder to support your growing child. And because of changes in your body's collagen, your joints are a bit more elastic, so be aware of back, knee, and ankle pain.

If you overheat, so does your baby, which can be dangerous, particularly during the first trimester. "Be very cautious about riding hard in hot weather," says Camilla Buchanan, M.D., an obstetrician/gynecologist in Williamsburg, Virginia. Avoid hot times of the day, ride easily, and drink more. You'll also dissipate heat more efficiently if you've been riding regularly before pregnancy.

Exercise will become harder during your third trimester—a hint to slow down. "Most women voluntarily cut back because they're uncomfortable," says Dr. Buchanan.

You're also overdoing it if you don't gain weight at the rate that your doctor recommends.

What if I crash? In a word, don't. Avoid all situations that increase the risk of a fall. These include big groups, pacelines, technical single-track and descents, and racing. "If you're pushing yourself hard, you'll make mistakes," says Dr. Buchanan, herself a competitive cyclist.

ACOG guidelines say to avoid any exercise during the third trimester that can cause even mild abdominal trauma. This certainly includes falling off your bike. Instead, consider pedaling indoors on a resistance trainer, or take up walking during those last few weeks. Even a minor fall could cause separation of the placenta, so if you do crash—especially in the last 20 weeks—get checked by your doctor immediately.

What should I eat and drink? "It's extremely important that women don't become dehydrated during exercise while they're pregnant," says Susan I. Barr, Ph.D., professor of nutrition at the University of British

Columbia in Vancouver. Dehydration can decrease blood flow and increase your core body temperature—both potentially dangerous for your child.

Swigging an extra bottle while riding isn't enough, says Beth Carlton, R.D., a registered dietitian, who advises, "Think in terms of prevention." Drink two or three glasses of water 2 hours before you ride. On the bike, use a sports drink or half-strength juice, which is absorbed into your bloodstream faster than water. Down at least 8 ounces every 20 minutes. Carry extra water bottles or get a backpack hydration system. This will hold up to 90 ounces and has a tube so you can sip continuously.

If you're drinking enough on and off the bike, you'll need to urinate often and your urine should be clear. Don't use thirst as a gauge. "By the time thirst arrives, you've already lost 1 percent of your body weight in fluid, which is 2 to 3 cups," says Carlton.

As for food, carbohydrate is your body's preferred fuel. Carlton says you need plenty to avoid dipping into the protein stores that your baby needs for development. Good mealtime carbs include bread, pasta, grains, fruits and starchy vegetables. If you're riding longer than an hour, nibble during the ride. Good choices include bananas, low-fat cookies, and fig bars.

According to Melpomene research, few expectant exercisers meet their vitamin and mineral requirements through food alone, so you'll likely need supplements. Your doctor can advise you.

How can I make cycling more comfortable? Balancing with a big belly won't be a problem for experienced cyclists, says Dr. Buchanan, noting that "your change in center of gravity occurs gradually and you easily adapt." But here are some ways to make cycling easier on you and your baby.

- Sit more upright by raising your handlebar as your belly expands. If necessary, install a taller stem or a mountain bike bar with an upward bend.

- A regular saddle that supports you well should work fine during pregnancy, too. But if changes in riding posture cause discomfort, consider a seat that's a bit wider or more padded.

- For stability, ride a hybrid or mountain bike, or put wider tires on your road bike. For easy and safe dismounts, you may also want to shelve your clipless pedals in favor of the old standard type. Ride without toeclips and straps, or at least keep the straps loose.

■ Because they bear more weight, pregnant women may have a tendency to get carpal tunnel syndrome, so use well-padded gloves and shift hand positions frequently.

■ If you ride a resistance trainer, do it in a cool room with a fan to prevent overheating. Keep plenty of water within reach.

Lessons from the Kid

I spent 8 years wrestling with whether I could give up cycling for the time that it would take a baby to develop (not to mention having my riding time jeopardized for years afterward). Whenever I cuddled my friends' progeny, my female hormones would scream at me to have a baby. I would torment myself with indecision until I was back on my bike and remembered how much I loved to ride.

During every cycling season of those 8 years, I also reentered the expert class of mountain bike racing. I never got much faster or stronger, but I always fantasized that one day I'd move up to the pro ranks. After enough ticks of the clock, reality set in. A child would always be with me. A racing career would not.

Each trimester brought its own set of trials. My first 3 months were marked by such fatigue that cycling wasn't an option. I struggled to walk two laps around the mile-long fitness loop near my home. I'd always considered walking as just a way of getting from one place to another. Now, I was writing it in my training log.

During the second trimester, winter forced me onto an indoor treadmill. Still not riding, I vowed to increase my walking to a jogging pace. And I did—up to a blistering 4 mph.

The third trimester and spring arrived at about the same time. Although I'd been cautioned to ease up during the final 3 months, I aspired to match the heroics of former national-team racer Miji Reoch, who secured her place in cycling lore by riding throughout her pregnancy and pedaling to the hospital while having labor contractions.

My first ride covered 6 miles. My husband pushed me not only up hills, but on the flats as well, where I would straighten up enough to inhale a few good breaths. How demoralizing. But I persevered.

■ Stick to less traveled roads with wide shoulders or bike lanes, or use bike paths if they're not congested with unpredictable kids and pedestrians.

Remember that the amount of fitness you lose by tempering your riding during these 9 months is minor and temporary—and a small price to pay for the peace of mind that comes from knowing that you're protecting your little passenger.

With a taller stem to accommodate my growing girth, I rode into the eighth month. I felt like another Miji. I would ride, pop out the baby, and get right back in the saddle again. I even fantasized about racing a few laps of an upcoming team mountain bike race—a mere month after the baby was due.

Then we went for the 34-week checkup. After measuring me, the midwife looked at me closely. "What have you been up to?" she asked. "Your uterus has shrunk 4 centimeters. It's supposed to have grown at least 2 more."

I was stunned into silence, too embarrassed to confess how much I had been riding. My husband had to tell her. Further exercise was banned, and I was sentenced to two extra protein shakes per day until the baby showed growth. I felt guilty for any harm I might have caused our child, but depressed about having my cycling curtailed. Fortunately, maternal guilt was stronger.

By the next appointment, my measurements were okay, but I'd learned my lesson. I no longer fooled myself with fantasies that I'm something more than I am. I'm no world-class racer or superwoman. I'm simply a reasonably fit human. Because I am fit, I thought I could ignore the guidelines on exercise during pregnancy, increasing my activity at a time when most pregnant women taper or stop. I'd let my ego lead the way instead of listening to the advice of experienced midwives. In my racing career, I had been unable to accept my limitations. But they hit home in one scary moment during pregnancy.

Now I understand why some riders get gold medals while I receive something less. More important, I accept it. But even though I can never match the pros on a bike, the healthy birth of my daughter, Emily, proved that there's at least one thing I can do as well as anyone.

By Carlotta Cuerdon

18

Make a Muscle

BY DELAINE FRAGNOLI

You're climbing a steep hill, standing and mashing the pedals for all you're worth. It's hard, but your legs feel like they can make it. The problem is, your bike is weaving all over the road. Or, you're on your mountain bike descending a rough, twisting singletrack. By the time you reach the bottom, your arms and hands are so tired that you dread every rock and rut in your path.

Normally you can keep up with the guys, but not now. What gives? In both scenarios, the culprits are a weak torso and arms. While women are not naturally blessed with great upper-body strength, biology—in this case—is not destiny. A little mid- and upper-body weight training can greatly increase your power and improve your cycling comfort and performance.

Balance of Power

The average woman has 56 percent of the upper-body strength of the average man, according to Christine Wells, Ph.D., author of *Women, Sport, and Performance: A Physiological Perspective*. This is due to a number of factors: our shorter torsos and arms, lower lean body mass (we have fewer and smaller muscle fibers and more body fat, resulting in a lower ratio of strength to weight), less of the hormone testosterone and, often, little experience in the weight room.

More important than our absolute or comparative strength is our uneven distribution of power. We are relatively strong in the legs and hips (women have about 72 percent of a man's strength) and weak in the abdominal region and arms. This has significant consequences when we ride. While we produce considerable torque with our legs, we some-times have trouble stabilizing our upper bodies and controlling our bikes' front ends, especially during power moves like out-of-the-saddle climbing and sprinting.

This strength discrepancy has other drawbacks. In cycling, 40 percent of your body weight should be supported by your upper body, points out Andrew Pruitt, Ed.D., director of Boulder Center for Sports Medicine in Colorado. A weak torso leads to incorrect riding position and early arm fatigue on long rides.

Dr. Wells concurs, noting that many women ride too heavy on the saddle—a recipe for saddle soreness and inefficient pedaling (it overworks the legs and underworks the powerful gluteus muscles). You need to have the strength to evenly distribute your weight on the handlebar, saddle, and pedals.

Dr. Pruitt adds that a weak upper body decreases your ability to absorb road (or trail) shock and to handle the effects of a fall.

In mountain biking, in particular, bike handling suffers. You may lack the power to pull up your bar enough to roll over a log, for example. As you become fatigued, steering gets sloppy and braking power diminishes.

Power Primer

The solution to these problems is simple and straightforward: Weight train your upper body. Just a little effort in this area can produce great results. "For women, a little bit of weight work does wonders," says Harvey Newton, a masters racer and a former U.S. Olympic weight-lifting coach.

While men and women respond to resistance weight training with similar strength and power gains (the major difference being that having less testosterone keeps women from bulking up), women should do a few things differently in the weight room. "A typical woman rider needs to spend a longer period of time working on maximum strength training (lifting greater weight with fewer repetitions) than most male cyclists would. She also needs to return to max strength training more frequently than the male does," says Joe Friel, a masters racer and cycling coach who has written one of the most respected books for serious riders, *The Cyclist's Training Bible*. Friel also recommends that women do some strength maintenance repeatedly throughout the season.

"It needs to be continual," Newton agrees.

Both Friel and Newton recommend a series of four multi-joint, cycling-specific exercises: seated rows, bench presses, crunches, and back extensions. Newton suggests that you work up to doing three sets of 6 to

12 reps, increasing the weight and the number of reps with each set until you reach about 80 percent of your maximum weight at the end of the final set. (Work with a certified fitness trainer at a reputable gym to determine your maximum lifting weight.) The first set can be a warmup set of 6 to 8 reps with light weight. The second set should include 8 to 10 reps at 60 percent. The final set should be 10 to 12 reps near 80 percent. Vary or change exercises every 4 to 6 weeks, select multi-joint exercises, and keep the workouts short.

Susan DeMattei's At-Home Workout

"I think that the best upper-body workout for mountain biking is mountain biking itself," says Olympic medalist Susan DeMattei. "Now that I'm not racing, I lack the strength that came from pulling on the handlebar while climbing, maneuvering on singletrack, and holding on during the descents."

Although she has weight trained in the past, DeMattei now favors exercises that she can do at home. "It's so expensive and time-consuming to go to the gym," she says, "and it can be intimidating." Her recommendations include pushups (start on your knees, then toes, and eventually "you can work up to doing them with a chair or stool" with your feet above your head); pullups ("This is good for your arms. A lot of women complain that their arms are flabby and this helps with the biceps"); and crunches ("I'm a crunchaholic. I do normal crunches, crunches to the side, crunches with my legs up in the air, all kinds of crunches. I find that it really helps alleviate my lower-back pain. Crunches also tone the muscles in the abs, which helps with that little pooch that a lot of cyclists get in the front of the stomach").

In addition to the exercises described above, DeMattei regularly works out with rubber bands. "They're great to take with you when you're traveling," she says.

Here are some of the exercises that DeMattei's friend Jane Tunnadine, a certified fitness trainer, recommends for upper-body strength training.

Abdominal crunches with a resistance band (targets abdominals). Lie in a supine position with your hands on either side of your body and hold the resistance band across your thighs. Lift your shoulders off the floor and try to bring your knees closer to your shoulders by lifting your hips. Breathe out as you crunch. Keep pressing the rubber band across your thighs during the exercise. Try two or three sets of 15 to 30 repetitions.

Back hyperextension (targets lower back). Lie in a prone position looking down at the ground. Place your palms down, under your face. Keep your hips, knees, and toes on the floor. Lift your arms and shoulders off the ground. Breathe out as you lift your shoulders. Do not look up. Try two or three sets of 15 to 30 repetitions.

Upright row (targets upper back and shoulders). Stand on the center of the rubber band with one foot. Keep your knees slightly bent and stand erect. Grip the handles of the band with your fingers facing your body. Pull both handles up toward your shoulders. Your hands should be shoulder-width apart. Your elbows will lead the movement and the exercise stops when your elbows are at shoulder level. Try two or three sets of 10 to 15 repetitions.

Biceps curl (targets biceps). Stand as above. Keep your arms close to your body during the exercise. Using your elbows as a pivot point, curl the handles up as far as you can. Do not let your wrists hyperextend during the movement. Try two or three sets of 12 to 15 repetitions.

Lateral shoulder raise (targets shoulders). Stand as above. Keeping slight bends in your elbows, raise both arms to shoulder level. Your hands, elbows, and shoulders should all be aligned at the end of the movement. You can also perform this exercise one arm at a time. Try two or three sets of 10 to 12 repetitions.

Triceps extension (targets triceps). Stand with your knees slightly bent and your body upright. Hold the band in one hand and place that hand firmly against your opposite shoulder just below your collarbone. Hold the end of the band in the other hand with your elbow bent. Using the elbow joint as a pivot point, extend your arm down the side of your body. Keep your elbow close to your side throughout the exercise. Repeat this exercise with the other arm. Try two or three sets of 10 to 12 repetitions.

Seated row (targets mid- and upper back and shoulders). From a seated position with the band under your feet, pull both handles back toward the sides of your body, squeezing your shoulder blades together. Do not rock back and forth with your upper body. Try two or three sets of 12 to 15 repetitions.

19

Love Your Butt

BY DELAINE FRAGNOLI

Perhaps no part of a woman's anatomy suffers more self-scrutiny than her butt. "Too big" and "too flabby" is our collective hue and cry. And letting it all hang out on bike rides in leave-little-to-the-imagination spandex shorts doesn't do much to alleviate our cracked rear view.

But if we can stop judging the appearance of our backsides long enough to understand their anatomy and cycling physiology, we can find many reasons to appreciate the locomotive uses of our cabooses. In what may be the ultimate exercise of mind over matter, you can learn to love your butt, build it right, and use it to your advantage.

Posterior Primer

Your butt is the seat of your cycling power, so to speak. Among the largest and strongest of all muscle groups, the gluteals in your rump aid hip extension and rotation, helping you initiate strenuous movements like climbing stairs, squatting, and pedaling.

Much of the power of each pedal stroke comes from the gluteus maximus, which comes into play in a major way through the first 90 degrees of each push. Two other buttocks muscles, the gluteus medius and gluteus minimus, provide balance during side-to-side weight shifts, such as when you're steering a bike—the lone case where a bum steer is a good thing.

We're designed to bear children, so it's our pelvic structure, rather than our musculature, that makes our butts look and work differently from men's butts. While each woman is shaped a bit differently, in general, a female pelvis is wider (relative to shoulder width) and more shallow than a male pelvis. Women's pelvises also tend to tilt at a greater angle. This increases the curve in our lower backs and makes our buttocks jut out more. Our backsides also seem larger than men's because we tend to store more fat in our hips and buttocks than they do. Blame it on that darn childbearing thing.

Speaking of childbearing, our pubic arches are wider (usually greater than 90 degrees, while men's are less than 90 degrees). This means that our ischial tuberosities or "sit bones"—the two main points that contact a bike seat—are farther apart. Also, our sit bones angle outward more, which contributes to this gender gap. This wider bone placement is why saddles won't support us correctly unless they're broader at the back.

Position Precision

Even the slightest anatomical differences between women and men can have significant effects on cycling comfort and performance. "Exactly what muscles you use, and when, will vary," says Andrew Pruitt, Ed.D., director of Boulder Center for Sports Medicine in Colorado. "Activation of specific gluteal muscles depends on pelvic shape and size, the position of your pelvis over the bike's crankset, riding position, and bike setup—particularly saddle adjustment."

Here's the rub. Our "butt jut" rolls our pelvises forward on the saddles and weights our soft tissues. Long top tubes and rangy stems exacerbate the problem, forcing us even farther forward onto our genitals. Add to this our wider pubic arches and outward-angled sit bones, and it's no wonder that many women suffer untold torture when riding hard-nosed, skinny-tailed saddles on bikes sized for men.

Other aspects of our anatomy also affect riding posture. For instance, because of our relatively larger hips and butts, our strength and center of gravity are naturally distributed rearward. "Women, in general, sit more on their butts. They're heavy on the seat," says Christine Wells, Ph.D., author of *Women, Sport, and Performance: A Physiological Perspective.* "I tell them that cycling is not a sitting sport."

The short, high-rise stems that many women prefer, often as compensation for improper bike fit or poor upper-body strength, encourage this upright, anchored-to-the-saddle riding style. While it may temporarily seem more comfortable, in the long run this butt-heavy position can increase saddle soreness. Compared to leaning farther forward, sitting too upright is also apt to overwork the legs and underwork the glutes—a waste of muscle power.

Such a riding position adversely affects bike handling as well. Uneven, rearward weight distribution can compromise steering and handling. (Sit up straight the next time you climb a steep pitch, and you'll see how hard it is to keep the front wheel pointed ahead.) Double-check that your position is properly balanced by reviewing the guidelines in chapters 11 and 12.

Despite its strengths, however, your butt is not without its weak points. Dr. Pruitt notes that our wider hips cause our thigh bones to angle more when they connect our hips to our knees. This increases the angle at which the top of each femur fits into the hip, making us more prone to gluteal tendinitis, hip bursitis, and overuse injuries to our wide-hip-induced "knock" knees. Again, the way to limit the risks is to make sure your riding position is correct.

The Bottom Line

Now that you know what your butt can and can't do for you, what can you do for your butt? How can you better harness your seat of power and help it look and work its best?

If you're riding your bike, you're already improving your butt. "Next to cross-country skiing, cycling is probably the best exercise for the buttocks," says Dr. Pruitt, who has served as the medical coordinator for the national cycling team.

While it's "physiologically impossible," in Pruitt's words, to spot reduce, cycling coupled with sound nutrition can lead to overall weight loss. Stick with it, and you'll have a much better chance of transforming those "buns of puddin'" into "buns of steel."

You can further tone your hips and buttocks—and increase your strength and cycling performance—with weight training. Exercises for the glutes, abdominals, and lower back can improve your sprinting, climbing, and balance. Many women are reluctant to do lower-body weight training for fear that their butts will get even bigger. Relax. Several decades of research show that while women make similar strength gains as men while lifting weights, we lack the hormones to increase bulk.

Now that we have our worries behind us, let's move on to which exercises work best. "I favor multi-joint exercises that closely simulate the movements of cycling: stepups, squats, leg presses, and dead lifts," says Joe Friel, a masters racer and cycling coach who has written one of the most respected books for serious riders, *The Cyclist's Training Bible.*

Dr. Pruitt recommends that women do standing hip extensions as well. Work with a certified instructor at your local gym or health club to learn the proper techniques for these exercises.

In addition, strength training your upper body develops the muscles needed for an efficient riding position so you can use your butt to its best advantage. With a stronger upper body, a more forward-reaching position (within the limits of genital crunching) can be attained. A bent-forward position improves aerodynamics (more speed with the same effort), climbing efficiency (more gluteal muscle recruitment), and uphill bike handling (especially off-road); and it reduces the potential for saddle soreness by putting a bit more of your weight on the handlebar.

Finally, remember that the mind is stronger than the butt. On the bike, concentrate on the positive. Think of all the power and balance that your glutes give you. Visualize them getting stronger and you getting faster. See your butt. Be your butt. Love your butt.

20
Now, about Your Diet

BY VIRGINIA DEMOSS

With all of the conflicting advice that's going around, probably the only women who aren't confused about nutrition are those of us who haven't been paying attention. After all, we're regularly bombarded with claims that some food or diet will help us live longer, lose weight, look younger . . . even ride better.

If you're tired of feeling perplexed—and perhaps bouncing from one food fad to another, only to learn the hard way that radical eating plans, magic ingredients, and expensive supplements don't work—this chapter is for you. It contains all you need to know about eating for good health and better cycling performance. No hype or empty promises, just the facts.

The Importance of Carbohydrate

If you had a plate of pasta for every article ever written about carbohydrate, you could start your own Italian restaurant. There's good reason, however, why sports nutritionists hype carb: It's your best fuel.

Essentially, carbohydrate is sugar. Simple carbohydrate is a single or double sugar molecule—usually glucose, fructose, galactose, sucrose, or lactose. These are found in nutritious foods (fruits, for instance) as well as in less healthful fare, such as candy. Complex carbohydrate is a long chain of simple sugars and is often called a starch. Potatoes and pasta are good examples.

When you eat carb, it's broken down and converted to blood glucose, your body's main fuel and the only type that can feed your brain. Glucose that's not immediately used for energy is stored in your muscles and liver as glycogen and used later for fuel. If these storage spots are full, the glucose is converted to fat.

Carbohydrate is a better cycling fuel than protein or fat. Although stored protein can be converted to energy when glucose and glycogen become depleted, the process is inefficient. Stored fat can also be a fuel source, but it can't be converted to energy in the absence of glucose. This is why you need carbohydrate. Not only does a diet that's high in fat and protein carry more calories and adverse health effects, it does a poorer job of providing energy for cycling.

During and immediately after a hard effort, simple and complex carb is equally effective as fuel. But in your general diet, it's best to emphasize the complex type, which promotes significantly greater glycogen synthesis and offers vitamins, minerals, and fiber along with the energy.

Carb Calculations

Overall, nutritionists recommend that at least 60 percent of your calories come from carbohydrate. For cyclists and other aerobic athletes, 65 percent is better. Food packages list carb content as a percentage of daily calories, making this fairly simple to track. To help, here's a formula that enables you to estimate the number of carb grams that you need to account for 65 percent of your diet.

First, determine your total calorie requirement by multiplying your weight by 15. To this number add 8 calories (10 for men) for each minute of cycling you do a day. The total is roughly the number of daily calories you need to maintain your weight. (To lose weight, consume 500 fewer calories each day. You'll lose 1 pound per week.)

For example, a 130-pound woman who does a 1-hour training ride would figure as follows: 130 × 15 = 1,950 calories + 480 calories (60 minutes × 8 calories) = 2,430 total calories. For this rider, 65 percent of total calories amounts to about 1,580 (2,430 total calories × 0.65 = 1579.5). This is the number of carb calories she should eat daily. Because carb has 4 calories per gram, she can divide 1,580 by 4 to determine that she needs about 395 grams of carb per day.

Beyond the math, the point is that you should increase your intake of whole-grain breads, nonfat dairy products, cereals, pasta, rice, potatoes, vegetables, fruits, and juices. At the same time, keep your total daily calorie consumption at the right level by decreasing your intake of fat and protein as found in meat, cheese, whole dairy products, and snack foods.

Beating the Bonk

No matter how well-trained you are, your endurance is limited by one thing: the depletion of stored glycogen. When glycogen is depleted, you become light-headed, dizzy, and fatigued. In cycling, we call it bonking. Fortunately, it isn't inevitable. There are ways to increase your glycogen stores and prolong performance.

The best way is through training. Well-conditioned muscles can store 20 to 50 percent more glycogen than untrained ones. To take advantage of this expanded capacity, you need to eat plenty of carb calories every day. Successive days of low intake can lead to a condition called training glycogen depletion, characterized by fatigue and lackluster performance.

For several days before an important event, pack your muscles with glycogen by reducing your riding and increasing your intake of carbohydrate to as much as 75 percent of total calories. By making more glycogen available to your muscles—and using less—you'll top off your tank for the big ride. If you have trouble consuming enough food to get all the carbohydrate you need, try a concentrated sports drink known as a carbo-loader, which can supply more than 200 grams of carbohydrate per serving.

Drinking Your Energy

Even the world's strongest cyclist would run out of gas if she didn't refuel while riding. The reason is simple. Early in a ride, almost all of your energy comes from stored muscle glycogen. But as glycogen levels decline, you rely more on blood glucose for fuel. To continue riding, you need to keep these sugar levels high.

One way to do this is with an energy drink. If a drink contains too much carbohydrate, however, it bogs down in your stomach and takes too long to reach your bloodstream, resulting in dehydration and possibly nausea. The most effective drinks contain just enough carbohydrate (5 to 7 percent) to empty into your bloodstream quickly, extending performance without interfering with hydration.

Some cyclists can drink fruit juice (perhaps diluted with water) or use commercial drinks with high (up to 25 percent) carb concentrations without problems. The benefit is a bigger dose of energy per bottle. When preparing a drink, you may want to try different concentrations to find the strongest one that causes no problems. Of course, experiment during training rides, not in important events.

To be effective, an energy drink should deliver about 40 to 60 grams of carbohydrate per hour. Check the ingredients and consider avoiding products that contain fructose (many do). This is a slow-absorbing sugar that causes stomach distress in some riders. Look instead for sucrose, glucose, or glucose polymers. The last consist of several glucose molecules linked together. This chain is absorbed quickly, as if it were a single molecule, but it breaks up in your bloodstream to give you the benefit of several glucose molecules instead of just one.

For rides longer than 2½ to 3 hours, you also want solid food. There are numerous commercial energy bars to choose from, plus good high-carb foods such as bagels, fig bars, bananas, or dried fruit. Unlike drinks, these choices do not enhance hydration. Drink plenty of water with them.

Fat Facts

Next to carbohydrate, fat is your body's best fuel. It's particularly useful on long, steady rides when intensity is low. But don't assume that this gives you license to eat all the ice cream and french fries you want.

True, body fat is important for storing vitamins and providing insulation. But in excess, it's one of the biggest health risks imaginable. It increases susceptibility to heart disease, high blood pressure, certain cancers, and diabetes.

We all have plenty of stored fat and, in fact, most of us have too much. While we can store only limited amounts of glycogen, we can stockpile unlimited fat. Remember, though, that fat can be burned only in the presence of glucose. For these reasons, what we need is more carbohydrate, not more fat.

Any kind of food can turn into body fat if you eat too much. But not surprisingly, the most likely source of body fat is dietary fat. Compared with protein and carbohydrate, dietary fat has more than twice as many calories (nine per gram rather than four), and it appears to be stored more readily.

For optimal health and performance, nutritionists recommend that you derive no more than 30 percent of your total calories from fat, and no more than 10 percent from the saturated fats found primarily in animal products. The remainder should be the unsaturated form that comes from vegetable oils, nuts, and grains.

One way to ensure a low fat intake is to check nutrition labels and select foods with less than 3 grams of fat per 100 calories. If this information isn't plainly listed, you can calculate the fat percentage this way: Look on the label for the grams of fat per serving. Multiply this number by nine, then divide the result by the calories per serving. The result is the percentage of calories from fat. For example, one serving of a popular cheese spread has 80 calories and 6 grams of fat. So, 6 grams of fat $\times$ 9 calories per gram of fat = 54 fat calories; and 54 fat calories $\div$ 80 total calories = 67.5 percent calories from fat. (To figure a food's percentage of calories from carbohydrate or protein, multiply the number of grams by four instead of nine. Then divide by total calories.)

Trim fat from your diet by reducing your intake of animal foods. When you do consume them, select lean cuts of meat, skinless poultry, and nonfat dairy products. You should also cut down on butter and margarine, salad dressings, and hydrogenated and tropical oils (prevalent in many baked goods).

Interestingly, the fitter you are, the better you burn fat. A well-trained body is capable of delivering more oxygen into the muscles, thus increasing the rate of fat metabolism and sparing some glycogen stores.

The Right Way to Reduce

Looking for long-term weight loss that will improve your cycling performance? Then trash the crash diets. Sure, some weight (mostly water and lean body mass) may come off quickly, but it usually returns just as fast.

To take off fat—and keep it off—you must make two permanent (and almost painless) lifestyle commitments. The first is easy: exercise. Make time to ride. Don't let yourself go more than 2 days without it. Studies show that you can stay trim with as little as 3 hours of exercise per week.

The second commitment is harder: Cut calories. The best way isn't eating less, but reducing fat intake. In the average American diet, nearly 40 percent of all calories come from fat. Trim this to 20 to 30 percent, and you're almost guaranteed to lose weight.

Remember, fat is twice as calorie-dense as protein or carbohydrate. So as long as your foods aren't fatty, you can eat plenty and still keep your calorie intake relatively low. For example, in a study at Cornell University in Ithaca, New York, subjects were put on either a 40 percent or 15 percent fat diet and allowed to eat all they wanted. Both groups ate similar amounts, but those in the 15-percent group averaged 700 fewer daily calories.

Protein Precautions

Cyclists do require more protein than sedentary people. But this doesn't mean you have to increase your protein intake. In fact, you're probably already getting more than you need.

One reason that cyclists need extra protein is for fuel. Once muscles have depleted their primary energy source (carbohydrate), they begin

Cycling and Burning Calories

How many calories does cycling burn? That's a tough question. All the variables that can occur during a ride—uphills, downhills, headwinds, tailwinds—plus the type of bike you're riding, the surface you're on, and the speed you're going can cause swings in calorie consumption.

Still, weight-conscious cyclists want to know. This chart, developed for *Bicycling* magazine by James Hagberg, Ph.D., professor of kinesthesiology at the University of Maryland in College Park, answers the question for the most significant variable: speed. It's well-known that the energy used in cycling varies dramatically as wind resistance changes. Simply choose your average speed, multiply your body weight by the coefficient for that speed, and you'll have a close approximation of the number of calories that you burn per minute.

Going uphill adds to the energy cost. Coasting downhill burns no extra calories, of course, but the combination of going up and then down always uses more energy than riding on flat ground. In general, add an additional 20 calories for every 100 feet of elevation gain during a ride (an average value for a cyclist and bike with a combined weight of 150 pounds).

using protein. "Protein can be a small but significant source of energy—about 5 to 10 percent of total energy needs," according to researcher Michael J. Zackin, Ph.D., of the University of Massachusetts Medical School in Worcester. "Protein calories become increasingly important in carbohydrate-depleted states. If you train more than an hour a day and begin to deplete glycogen stores, you become increasingly dependent on body protein for energy."

Though results vary widely, Dr. Zackin says that cycling may raise your protein requirements 20 to 90 percent beyond the U.S. Recommended Dietary Allowance (RDA). The RDA is 0.363 grams of protein per pound of body weight. For a 130-pound woman, this is about 47 grams per day. Add the 20 to 90 percent, and the daily protein need rises to 56 to 89 grams.

That may seem like a lot, but most active people are already at these levels or beyond. This was illustrated in a study of eight highly trained women cyclists. Though their diets fell short of recommended values for several nutrients, their protein intake was 145 percent of the RDA. High protein levels simply aren't hard to reach. For instance, 3 ounces of

CALORIE CONSUMPTION

AVG SPEED (MPH)	COEFFICIENT (CAL/LB/MIN)
8	0.0295
10	0.0355
12	0.0426
14	0.0512
15	0.0561
16	0.0615
17	0.0675
18	0.0740
19	0.0811
20	0.0891
21	0.0975
23	0.1173
25	0.1411

meat, fish, or poultry contains 21 grams of protein. A cup of beans has 14 grams, 3 tablespoons of peanut butter has 12, and a cup of nonfat milk contains 9. All of this adds up quickly. In fact, the average American consumes 100 grams of protein per day.

So unless you're a strict vegetarian or chronic dieter, you probably don't need to increase your protein intake. Instead, worry about where your protein comes from. The best sources are low in fat and include a healthy dose of complex carbohydrate. Muscles are built by work, not extra protein, and work is best fueled by carbohydrate.

Some low-fat, high-protein choices include whole grains, beans, vegetables, fish, skinless poultry, soy products, lean cuts of meat, and nonfat dairy products. Even vegetarians can get plenty of high-quality protein with a varied diet combining grains, legumes, nuts, seeds, vegetables, dairy products, and eggs.

Overall, nutritionists say that about 15 percent of your diet should be protein calories. But don't sweat it. This is one nutrition goal that you'll reach without even trying.

Do You Need Supplements?

If you're eating a well-balanced diet, you almost certainly get all of the vitamins and minerals that you need. A cyclist's vitamin and mineral requirements are no greater than those of a sedentary person, according to nutritionist Ellen Coleman, author of *Eating for Endurance*. "Remember, vitamins do not provide a direct source of energy. Their only purpose is to help people with nutritional deficiencies stemming from poor diets."

No research has found that taking supplements improves performance in well-nourished cyclists. On the other hand, some substances can actually accumulate in the body to dangerous levels if taken in large quantities. Too much niacin, for example, can cause rashes, nausea, and diarrhea. It can also interfere with your body's ability to burn fat for fuel. This forces you to use glycogen at a faster rate, with makes you fatigue quicker during a ride.

At about a dime per pill, a daily vitamin/mineral supplement is often viewed as cheap insurance. So go ahead if you want to be sure that all bases are covered. But if you're feeling tired or your performance is slipping, don't expect supplements to help. The cause is probably too much training or eating too little carbohydrate, not the lack of some vitamin.

"When people feel better after taking vitamin and mineral supplements, it's usually due to the strength of their belief that they'll help—the placebo effect," Coleman notes.

21

Key Questions Answered

BY MEMBERS OF *BICYCLING* MAGAZINE'S
FITNESS ADVISORY BOARD

Training. Fitness. Health. Nutrition. All of these topics are essential to good performance in cycling. In this chapter are answers to a wide range of questions from women, covering many areas of concern that may help you understand and solve similar problems that you may encounter.

Q: *What's the best way to make sure I improve as a cyclist?*

A: It may be as simple as keeping a training diary—and then using it to learn what helps you improve so you can repeat it (while avoiding methods that aren't effective), according to Elaine Mariolle, former winner of the Race Across America (RAAM).

During the year before her RAAM victory, Mariolle combined speed workouts with endurance training, an effective combination that can benefit any rider. She recommends using "a reliable cyclecomputer that calculates average miles per hour in tenths. This lets you measure your progress accurately and compare performances over the same route." Record your daily training data, plus notes about how you feel, what you ate, the weather, or any other factor that plays a role in the ride. Tally your miles for each week and month. Reading the diary later, you'll be encouraged by your improvement and see patterns that led to periods of strong riding.

Your diary will also help you plan in the future. For example, if you ride 2,500 miles this year without undue fatigue, you can confidently push to 3,000 next year—even if you don't do them all at once in RAAM.

Don't become a slave to those blank pages, though, and ride only to keep filling in numbers. "My philosophy is that you don't ride just in order to go faster or farther," says Mariolle. "You should have a good time, too. By keeping it fun, I think most people will surprise themselves with how good they can get."

Q: *I'm about 50 pounds overweight and haven't been on a bike since I was a child. I want to start cycling for fitness and pleasure but don't know where to begin. What do you suggest for a terribly out-of-shape 30-year-old woman?*

A: Start by adopting a high-carbohydrate, low-fat diet. Omit fried foods and baked goods, add lots of fresh fruits and vegetables, and eat red meat sparingly. Consult a dietitian in your area.

As for training, I suggest riding in an easy gear. Spin the pedals against low resistance. Set a goal of cycling 10 miles in 1 hour on a road bike. If you're riding a mountain bike with knobby tires or a hybrid with an upright riding position, you should try for 7 or 8 miles. Then gradually increase your speed and distance—about 2 miles each jump—as you become fit.

Two common mistakes made by beginners are trying to keep pace with more accomplished riders and pedaling in too high of a gear. So do your own thing at your own speed and enjoy yourself. Ride at least three times per week. Stick with it, and results will follow.

Q: *I'm a new rider who cycles to firm my legs, lose weight, and stay healthy. I ride 15 to 20 miles on 4 or 5 days per week. To reach my goals, should I be riding for speed or distance? And should I be cycling every day?*

A: Firming muscles, losing weight, and staying healthy are three popular exercise goals. To reach them, ride for speed *and* endurance. Your training week should include:

Moderate days. To lose weight, forget the clock and ride moderate distances at a comfortable pace. For a rider of your level, this should entail two to four rides per week of 15 miles. Such workouts burn fat without overstressing your body.

Endurance days. To improve your stamina, go on one long ride each week, say, 40 to 50 miles. Don't worry about time, just aim to go the distance. A weekend club ride would be great for this.

Speed days. These are key to cardiovascular improvement and muscle tone. Twice a week, try to average at least 15 mph on your road bike while maintaining a brisk pedaling rate (cadence) of 85 to 90 rpm. Gradually increase speed and duration as you become fitter.

This schedule lets you rest 1 day a week. Recovery is important for building strength. (If you ride the road on a mountain bike with knobby tires, reduce the mileage guidelines by about half.)

Q: *I start each season with goals and good intentions, but halfway through, I'm bored and slacking off. How can I avoid that?*

A: Variety is the answer. First, vary your route to transform tedious rides into new experiences. Second, don't just plug away. Vary your pace by sprinting for road signs, attacking the hills, or boosting your speed for a few minutes as if you were riding a time trial. On days when you lack motivation, remove the pressure to do a specific workout. Explore a new route and enjoy the scenery. At the end of the ride, you may find that you almost averaged training pace. If you didn't, maybe you've been overtraining and you need a break.

Third, join your local cycling club. Organized rides or training sessions with other cyclists are usually more exciting than going alone. Plus, you'll learn about different training techniques, riding styles, and equipment to enhance your overall progress.

Caution: Don't ride with stereo earphones in an attempt to beat boredom. They reduce your valuable ability to hear what's going on around you. In fact, many states outlaw them because they've contributed to accidents.

Q: *Help! I'm uncertain whether I need a heart-rate monitor. How important are they to someone just starting out?*

A: A heart-rate monitor (HRM) can be a valuable training device. With systematic use, you'll progress faster to a higher fitness level. If you're serious about becoming a good rider, it's a worthwhile investment of $90 (and up).

A HRM typically consists of a wristwatch-style monitor and a chest strap with electrodes. This strap uses radio waves to transmit your heart's electrical activity, which is then translated to beats per minute. This information is vital if you're following one of the popular training programs that require riding in certain heart-rate zones. The HRM helps you keep your heart rate in the range that's right for a given day's training. You won't go too easy and neither will you overextend yourself.

To burn fat and improve your aerobic ability without risking much stress to your body, ride at 55 to 65 percent of your maximum heart rate. At the other extreme, to improve your ability to ride fast and tolerate the painful buildup of lactic acid in your muscles, do short efforts with your heart rate pegged at 85 to 90 percent. (To find your maximum heart rate, wear your HRM, warm up well, then go all-out up a long, steep climb—and sprint at the top! Obtain your doctor's approval first, of course.)

Q: *I'd like to start training, but I don't want to commit to a complicated schedule of so-many-miles at such-a-speed each day. Is there some general advice I could follow?*

A: When I cook, I don't measure anything. I mix ingredients, taste it, and make changes. That's how training can work, too. You have a list of ingredients and you vary the recipe. The results will taste a little different for each cyclist.

Set some goals so you know how a given training week fits into the big picture of the whole year—or even the rest of your life. You can't control your work schedule, the weather, or your inherited talent. But you can control the thoughtful progression toward your goals. So get a big wall calendar with the whole year on it. Pencil in your rough goals and have a general idea of what you want to do each day to meet them.

Ten hours a week for training is a magical number for most serious riders. If you can train this much during each 7-day period, you can achieve most of your genetic potential. You'll have time to go hard but also to take some easy rides. If pressed for a suitable block of time, try doing two short rides a day. Go hard for an hour in the morning, then pedal easily after work to aid recovery and relieve the stress of the day.

Q: *What is overtraining and how do I avoid it?*

A: If you feel deeply fatigued for more than a day or so—your muscles ache, you're irritable, your appetite decreases, and your heart rate is elevated at rest or not responding normally during a ride—you're probably overtraining. Take a rest day, then cut your mileage and intensity until you feel like yourself again. Don't try to train through these symptoms, or you could suffer a significant setback.

Q: *I purchased a bike trailer so I could take my 1-year-old son on rides. At present, he can tolerate only an hour, which allows for 12 to 15 miles about five times a week. How can I get the most efficient workout within these time and mileage constraints?*

A: Pulling a trailer is a good workout. In hilly terrain, every pedal stroke can be like a leg press. The first priority is to install low gears, if you don't have them already. Your knees will thank you.

As for training methods, I don't recommend intervals or high-intensity regimens with a trailer. Such an approach will trash you, and the high speeds may endanger your child. Instead, think of a trailer ride as power training. It will develop muscle strength and may even contribute to time-trial performance, but it won't do much for your acceleration or leg speed. For that, you need to schedule time for riding without Junior and doing intervals or sprints. Perhaps you could do these at home on a stationary trainer.

As for your child, it's important to make the rides fun. Make the trailer into a veritable playhouse by loading in his favorite toys and plush animals. As he gets older, include books, food, and a water bottle. The longest ride that my wife and I generally take with our daughter is 2½ hours, and this includes a stop at a park. In general, think of the trailer as a family experience that provides training, not the reverse.

Q: *I seem to perspire very little compared with my cycling companions. In fact, on very warm days, I overheat and need to slow down. My doctor gave me a clean bill of health and said that my problem is due to individual differences. Should I be content riding in my club's 13-mph category, or is there something I can do to move up to 16 mph?*

A: Many women don't sweat as much as men. Instead, we rely on our cardiovascular systems to move body heat to the skin surface for dissipation. This works, but it can strain your system. This is what you're feeling when you say you have to slow down.

You should enhance your cardiovascular efficiency with a training program. Three times a week for 30 minutes or more, ride at about 75 percent of your maximum heart rate. (You can estimate your max by subtracting your age from 220.) Hold your heart rate at your 75 percent number, and the result will eventually be an increase in your blood volume and heat tolerance. In time, you should be able to join the 16-mph club.

Q: *Whenever I ride fast for long periods of time, my knees hurt. This doesn't happen when I ride slowly in a low gear. Last year, I rode 4,000 miles, including several 100-mile days. After this much training, shouldn't my knees be able to handle the strain?*

A: Your knee pain could stem from any number of physical problems, ranging from abrasion of tendons to roughness behind the kneecaps (chondromalacia). But even healthy knees can become sore if you're cycling improperly. Before subjecting yourself to the time and cost of a medical exam, try these possible solutions.

First, make sure your bicycle is properly adjusted. If still in doubt, consult a cycling coach or knowledgeable professional at a bike shop. Second, when riding, use moderate gears that allow you to spin the pedals at 80 to 95 rpm. Turning a big gear at a slow cadence can stress your knees. Third, rework your training schedule. Too many 100-mile days, especially if close together, may be taking their toll. Ride shorter distances, more often.

Q: *I rode my first century last year in less than 6 hours. But while training for it, my legs became large, and I wasn't able to reduce my waist measurement. Can I ride so my legs stay trim?*

A: Don't be afraid of developing a little size. You've discovered what may be true for many women—your previously unused leg muscles developed before you began to lose fat.

The best way to reduce your waist and not develop large legs is to do endurance riding all year. This means spinning with low pedal resistance and high revolutions (around 90 rpm). Aim for about 70 percent of your maximum heart rate. In this way, you'll burn plenty of calories, but you won't be doing high-intensity exercise that would increase muscle development.

If weight loss is your goal, remember that reducing fat in your diet is important. But don't skimp on calories when you're doing endurance cycling. Also, include some exercises that can help with toning, such as abdominal crunches to counteract the stomach "pooch" that cycling may bring on.

Meanwhile, rather than fret about slightly bigger legs, be proud of what they can do!

PART FIVE

Opportunities

22

Women's School for Roadies

BY PENNY PISANESCHI

Reasons varied, but each of us wanted one thing: to get more out of cycling. My roommate, Julie Sanchez, had recently upgraded her racing category and thought a week-long road camp—the first for women by renowned Olympic cyclists (now coaches) Connie Carpenter and Davis Phinney—would push her to a higher level. Two other women, friends from Colorado, came for an "active vacation." Another wanted to overcome her need for a granny gear. As for me, a beginning racer, I sought better cornering and bike-handling skills and to climb a "real mountain."

I would get my chance, surrounded as we were by the peaks above Sun Valley, Idaho. The camp was held during early summer in conjunction with a top stage race for women, the International Women's Challenge. A highlight for all 24 of us would be seeing how we compared with the pros in a time trial. But first we had friends to make and skills to learn during an intense-but-fun week of training and seminars.

Day 1: Aspirations

As we're divided into five groups of five or six women, Connie and Davis ask us to break the ice by telling about ourselves during a meeting the first evening. My group's coach, Ray Browning, is a professional triathlete with road racing experience. Skip Hamilton's group also consists of stronger riders who aspire toward road racing, time trials, ultramarathon cycling, and triathlons. He himself is a national-class cyclist, runner and cross-country skier. I'll spend most of my riding time with these two groups, but it's interesting to learn about the other women, too.

Day 2: Be Cool

My group's first ride is an easy 35 miles of spinning on the bike path to Bellevue. "Consider yourselves a team," instructs Coach Ray. "We want to become a well-oiled machine. Also, I'd like for us to think of a team name."

We roll out, and before long Davis rides up alongside. "So you're the lucky group that gets to watch Ray's butt for the next couple of days," he jokes. About this time, Skip's group flies past us. I see my roomie, Julie, in there and worry that my group might not be fast enough for me. I feel an urge to try to catch them. They're hammering. This camp is my first good opportunity to gauge myself against other women, and I want to prove myself.

But we keep riding at "conversation pace," discussing group riding etiquette and pacelines. Ray reminds us to keep our shoulders loose to relax the whole upper body, saving our energy until it's really needed.

In the paceline, we concentrate on maintaining the same speed when taking the front, rather than accelerating and opening gaps. Gradually, we ride closer to one another and become more efficient. We also get faster even though we're not working harder. It feels comfortable. We are becoming a "well-oiled machine." We are also gaining on Skip's team.

"How about 'Ray's Baybes' for our team name?" someone suggests. Cool, we think. Ray beams with pride.

Later that day, we move to a room in our hotel with resistance trainers and full-length mirrors. Each rider is instructed to mount her bike and spin easily. Once we're comfortable, our coach will make any necessary adjustments. "Cakewalk," I say to myself. I can hear Connie now: "Penny, you have the most ideal position of any rider I've ever seen." I board my racing machine and wait for the compliments to pour in. Ray points out that not only do I need a longer stem, but my saddle should go up and back. I'm told I have a quirky way of riding with my butt up in the air. "Oh, nice," I think.

Ray raises my saddle (spin, spin). I make Ray put it down (spin, spin). Ray moves my saddle back (spin, spin). I make Ray move it forward (spin, spin). Ray looks me square in the eye. "You're high maintenance, aren't you?" Ray gives up.

This enlightening day continues as we pedal to a church parking lot. Traffic cones form an obstacle course to ride through. I eagerly await our instructions. Hopeless at cornering, I've been avoiding the most common type of road race, the criterium, because I can't corner well enough to keep up. I want desperately to change that. While Davis describes the techniques, Skip rides to illustrate. His movements are so fluid that it's hard to break down what he's doing.

It isn't coming to me. Davis starts to explain all over again. Then Connie. I continue to try, but to no avail. Then I hear the other girls laughing. Apparently, my butt is sticking up again. Now I'm self-conscious as well as frustrated.

Finally, I ride directly behind Skip and try to mimic his moves around each cone. Skip yells, "Now!" at the instant I should start a turn. I follow him for about 10 minutes. Then it clicks. I feel it! A seamless flow around one cone and then the next, left turn, right turn. I practice until I'm the only one still in the lot. Criteriums, here I come.

Day 3: A Climb to Remember

We are scheduled to ride from Sun Valley to Stanley, where we'll eat lunch at Redfish Lake and watch the pro women finish a stage of the International Challenge.

Mountain weather changes these plans, however. It rains heavily all morning and it's snowing on the passes. Ray's Baybes and Skip's team decide to tough it out and ride a 60-miler anyway. Instead of going straight to Stanley and stopping, though, we'll climb Galena Summit and then ride back to camp, round-trip.

Galena Summit is the climb that will determine our camp's "Queen of the Hill." We leave Sun Valley in a cold, steady rain, with Ray's Baybes a few minutes ahead of Skip's group. We ascend steadily for 25 miles until we reach Galena Lodge 5 miles from the top. After a pit stop, we resume the climb. I want to be a "Queen" contender, but maybe even more I don't want any of Skip's riders to catch me.

I could lie and say this is a thrill, but I'm hurtin' bad. That little anaerobic-threshold demon inside my head is screaming, "You suck! Skip's group is gonna pass you. And you thought you could be a climber." I'm dropped by two fellow Baybes. I'm miserable. So I came to camp to "climb a real mountain." Ha!

Then a funny thing happens. I stop to peel off a layer of clothing and give myself a chance to stop wheezing. I forgive myself for being dropped. I take big breaths of crisp mountain air. The frozen rain lets up. The sun illuminates the pine-carpeted Sawtooth Mountains. I feel the warmth on my cheeks. I am climbing a real mountain.

I reach the top just before Susan, the first from Skip's group. As she rounds the last hairpin, sunshine seems to radiate from her eyes. Six months earlier, this woman had open-heart surgery and a pacemaker put in. She came to this camp, and this mountain, intent merely on "doing my best." Instead, she leads her team with an incredibly fast climb.

After the freezing descent, we form two pacelines for the ride back. It pours for the last 20 miles. We can hardly see the wheels in front of us. We push hard to keep warm and to get back fast. "Great pull!" we yell to one another. In no time we're sprinting like maniacs for the Sun Valley town line. It's over! No one says it, but we know we're tough. This is chick bonding at its best.

Day 4: Sprint School

An easy warm-up ride takes us to East Fork/Triumph. It offers great views of jagged, snowcapped mountains as well as a perfect loop for sprint lessons, with long, flat, straight stretches.

We gather to hear Davis reveal the techniques that won him two Tour de France stages and more road victories than anyone in U.S. racing history. His sprint tips: Develop upper-body strength to enhance power; keep shoulders and hips square with the bike; keep hands on the drops except on steep uphill sprints (grip the brake levers then); center body weight over the pedals (too far forward and the rear wheel can slip); position your butt so it almost touches the tip of the saddle; keep your head up.

He demonstrates ("It doesn't get any better than this," I reflect) and then it's our turn. I'm a little nervous, expecting a repeat of the cornering clinic. I'm prepared to get loads of additional advice to iron out my imperfections.

"Ready?" Ray asks. "Ready!" Umphh. Push. Push. Push. My hands are on the drops. My head is up. Power. Power. My body feels centered and my bike feels connected. For once, my butt is exactly where it's supposed to be, right at the nose of the saddle. One last pusssh. . . . Ray looks happy. "Your form was great, Penny. You have a good sprint." Really?

We cap this session with one more try, all of us together. I have a burning desire to do this right. Davis is watching. Then something unusual happens. I feel confident. I let Karyn and Aileen cut the wind while they watch each other. I relax. Coming into the final stretch, I feel for the moment. In position, I pounce around Aileen's left. No one reacts until it's too late. Hey, maybe I do have a sprint. Scary thought.

Day 5: Time Trialing with the Pros

Today we get the chance to compete against the pro women. Well, sort of. We will race the same 3.2-mile time trial course being used for the Challenge, to see how we measure up. Being a time trial, we each start alone at a set interval. There's no tactics now. It's just a matter of how fast each of us can complete the distance.

Ray is describing the course features. I look over and see Rebecca Twigg, Jeanne Golay and my idol, Laura Charameda, warming up. I can't believe I'm doing this.

Three . . . two . . . one . . . go! I'm out of the saddle and pushing hard to get up to speed. I've practiced ahead of time with different gears, and so far I'm flying. But here comes my anaerobic threshold and—oops!—there it goes. I see two women up the road and try to regain control by concentrating on reeling them in. When the course begins its 220 feet of climbing, I work even harder to make ground. They aren't getting any closer.

I feel pain. I start panting. The course gets steeper. Negative thoughts whirl through my head. I sense I'm being passed and look left. An experience like this can be demoralizing, but it's Susan who comes into view. Can you believe that this is a woman with a pacemaker? Her speed is inspiring. Her form is excellent. Her bike is humming. "Go, Susan!" I yell. I'm happy to be caught by only one person. I'm proud it's Susan.

Later, Ray takes each of us aside to review our camp experience. He tells me I have good speed on the flats, pretty good climbing ability, and the potential to be a good sprinter. He cautions that I tend to go for it all at once and blow up. I need more self-control. I tell him that I'll work on it, and I mean it.

Closing Ceremony

The festivities that conclude camp are bittersweet. Davis thanks us for our determination, our self-control in putting our competitive natures aside, and our support of each other. He commends our toughness and good attitude on that cold, wet day up to Galena Summit. He makes us feel part of something special.

Connie says, "This camp has been a dream come true for me." We all second that.

The staffers present many imaginative awards. There's "The Dinosaur Club" award for the oldest campers. Julie is dubbed "Most Stylin' Cyclist" for her fashion sense and good form. Aileen is crowned "Queen of the Hill" for her performance during the Galena Summit epic. Her award is a ceramic mug made by Connie herself.

Then Connie starts to describe the next award winner. She takes out a wind-up toy bicycle ridden by a girl in pigtails. "This cyclist has so much energy and enthusiasm, few can keep up with her," Connie explains, roasting this poor camper as the toy rider spins her little legs around and around. The room roars. I feel left out of a joke, then Julie glances at me. I break into a sweat.

"I'd like to present this award to the camp's youngest cyclist, all of 26. Penny, come up here." I begin to laugh so hard tears are forming. My prize is a pacifier. "It's not just for you," Connie says, "it's for the person on the plane home sitting next to you."

It was some camp, and you can bet that person heard all about it.

Penny Pisaneschi races on the roads and trails in Northern California, where she works in sales for a software company.

23
Playing Dirty

BY KATHY BURNS

Addiction to mountain biking knows no barriers. It strikes beyond the young, the thin, and the studly. I am rolling proof. One look will tell you I don't exactly match the archetype. As a 48-year-old "femme fossil," I will never be thought of as a climbing stick. There are so few racers like me competing that I barely ever have the luxury of an age bracket, much less a Clydesdale class for females. That leaves me in the perennial dust as the 20-something spring chickies sprint off in front of me. By race's end I'm generally a little further off the back each year, but I finish and finish and finish.

What possesses me? (Believe me, I ask myself this every race.) Mostly I feel proud. Proud, strong, and healthy, appreciated for my independence. If I ignore the creaks and the scar tissue, my body is vigorous and resilient. It seems I get in better shape each year.

I have to—I feel the pressure of the younger women coming up at me from the veteran class. Most of them are my friends and can bury riders far younger than they are. One did so last year while her twin 2-year-old granddaughters cheered her on. I was thrilled for her. There is a camaraderie among women mountain bikers: We're so glad to see any woman step up to the line that we tend to pull for each other.

Take the Nationals at Mount Snow, Vermont. My front wheel went out of true, rubbing the brake pads, seconds before my cross-country race. A competitor, Marcia MacDonald, noticed that I'd broken a spoke. She adeptly let out some cable to open my brake, then twisted the dead spoke around its nearest buddy. We howled at the absurdity, the unlikelihood of this ever happening in a men's race.

I soon settled into the gruesome task of pedaling up the 1,350-foot climb. Just as I gained the crest, my front tire collapsed, the brake having rubbed through the casing. So I ran and pushed and carried my steed through hippo-pits of mud. The sun-scorched, uphill climb nearly nailed me, but the crowd pulled me home. Amazingly, I was swept right into the announcer's booth and interviewed. Everyone heard my story. Three months later I earned my first national ranking from that assist, from that run. Second in the country—right behind Marcia.

There's no doubt in my mind: Attitude, toughness, and perseverance count just as much as speed.

The notion to mountain bike originated from an article my husband read when off-road rigs first started being made. He was convinced he had to try it and wanted to buy a bike. I insisted on parity. In a suburban parking lot, late in November on a day going dark, I circled around with no clue about how to shift. From there I quickly discovered dirt and later became a full-fledged "hammerette" on a drop-dead beautiful 50-mile ridge (called the Gunks in upstate New York) with cliffs and waterfalls, all laced with carriage roads.

Cycling soon became an outlet for all my cares and worries—right when I needed it most. My 23-year marriage went down, puncturing my reality. I found myself flat-out lonely, needing emotional repairs and a new direction. Mountain biking highlighted my self-sufficiency and gave me context.

Ultimately, we all have to ride our own ride. The bike helps me re-

Getting Started

If you'd like to try your legs at mountain racing, first check at a bike shop to learn about local training races and pick up flyers for upcoming events. If a race is sanctioned by the National Off-Road Bicycle Association (NORBA), you'll have to buy a 1-day racing license ($5) at the event. For more information, contact NORBA, One Olympic Plaza, Colorado Springs, CO 80909.

member that. When I wreck, I have to pick myself up and figure out how to keep going. As things break, including my body, I must learn how to fix them. It takes practice to pull your own weight. Soon I was mountain biking everywhere I could imagine— West Virginia, Utah, all over New England.

Then I found myself drawn to a local race. There I was awestruck by a woman I noticed across the infield. She was roughly my age, petite, and powerful beyond my comprehension. She introduced herself as Carol Waters and was enthusiastic about my trying competition. Then she went out and beat the knobbies off all the women in a time that rivaled the men's field. She became my hero, setting a standard of achievement for women over 40. When I came back for more the next year, Carol was there again cheering me on.

Later that summer I headed to Hunter Mountain for the New York State Championships. As I led my class up the mountain, some outrageous climber in the pack was relentlessly overtaking me. A tender voice said, "You're doing great, Kathy! Stay steady and ride your race. It's Carol. I'm just warming up." Here was my mentor, like a thunderbolt, coaching from my back wheel during my first championship. She became world veteran champion that year.

Even though I didn't win that race, 2 years later I was New England Sport Masters Champion. I was then able to dominate the series, and my goal became to move up to the expert class and qualify for the World Masters Team. Not bad for a pedalosaurus.

Kathy Burns achieved her goal of qualifying for the World Team and went on to compete in the World Championships.

24

It's Never Too Late

BY PHYLLIS COHEN

Race Across America, August 1996. About 2:00 A.M. on the sixth night of the race, somewhere in Tennessee, heading east on a narrow backwoods two-lane road, illuminated only by the headlights of the support van. A vertical climb with steep switchbacks slicing through overgrown summer vegetation and crickets so loud I was hallucinating that they were an entire extraterrestrial population. If I rode any slower, I'd tip over.

The inner voice hissed at me: "This is horrible. Quit. It's ridiculous to waste time at this pace. Get Celeste (my teammate) out here." Then out of that nowhere state of mind came an audible thought: "You didn't even say goodbye to me," and I burst into tears. In the middle of the night, slogging up a mountain on my bicycle, I was experiencing a flashback of emotion repressed from my mother's death, 36 years earlier. . . .

Up ahead, Celeste rested in the other van, waiting to take over for me. For the last 3 hours we'd been spelling each other at 45-minute intervals. We had another hour to go before our other two teammates would take over and let us get some rest. Theoretically, Celeste and I were linked by two-way radios and cell phones, but they didn't work in the mountains. And if they did, it wouldn't have mattered because only death was a good enough excuse for stopping. No kidding. We'd actually discussed it as we planned our strategy for this nonstop, 2,905-mile race called RAAM that had started in Irvine, California, and which we hoped to soon finish in Savannah, Georgia.

The headlights of the support van encased me in a forward-moving cocoon of light and ensured my safety. Somehow this engendered a mental state I came to think of as "bike as psychiatric couch"—a sort of free association of the road. Perhaps so much energy is used to keep going physically that there's none left to maintain defense mechanisms, so all kinds of bizarre thoughts and feelings bubble up. Maybe a solution to an old problem, maybe expansive feelings of blessedness, maybe long-repressed emotions, like the memory of my mother. The effect is cathartic, and you just keep on crankin' as hard as you can until you see the other van waiting up ahead or, most beautiful of RAAM sights, the motor home where you can finally get some sleep.

Who, Me?

This was not exactly what I'd envisioned 30 months earlier when Chris Kostman, then director of Team Race Across America, dangled the "you could set a world record" carrot and enticed me into trying to form a first-ever women's 50-plus senior team to compete in RAAM. My ego had been so happy; it waved flags at the very thought. After all, how many chances do you get to be first at anything? Besides, I'd been searching for years for something to inspire me to finally quit smoking forever. As I investigated RAAM, I realized that this was a serious undertaking that would change my life. Although I'd never competed in any sport, I believed that somewhere inside me was an athlete. RAAM was just what I needed, just when I needed it.

In reality, my transition from nice Jewish girl to endurance athlete had begun 11 years earlier, in 1985, with my father's death from cancer. My mother had died in 1960, also from cancer. During my father's illness, I kept hearing from doctors that I had to be "careful" because I was in a "high-risk group." What the doctors meant was frequent testing. To me that conjured up negative images of a waiting game. Instead, I resolved to be as healthy and physically fit as possible. It was not so much about living long as it was about living strong.

I had been doing aerobics and playing racquetball for years, but now I was on a mission. It didn't take long to learn that cardiovascular workouts are just part of the fitness picture. My first discoveries were weight training and nutrition.

Though progress with weights is slow, the rewards are amazing. In the first year you get "the look," but later there are deeper benefits of stress relief and a sort of physical confidence—a gut feeling that "this is a good body." Nutrition became important because it was obvious that what I ate one day directly affected my workout the next day.

After several years, I began to wonder what level of fitness would be possible if I really got dedicated. Going to bed early and getting up at dawn to train for 2 hours before work became the best way to start the day. I was training like a pro—except I was still smoking. I had stopped many times, but I'd always started up again.

Heartbeat Account

That's when I happened upon Johnny G's Spinning Center in Santa Monica, California. Driving by, I saw the sign, a neon wheel with the word "Spinning." Thinking it was a weaving store (a new shop!), I stopped in. Imagine my shock to find an indoor cycling workout in progress. Fifteen glistening bodies on stationary bikes were crankin' it to the pounding music. A wildly energetic and studly Johnny G, with his shoulder-length curly hair, was urging them on.

"Come on," he said to me, "you have to try this." I went home, changed into workout clothes, and went right back. Little did anyone know that this was the first of many Spinning Centers that would spring up across the country, introducing a popular new workout technique for the 1990s.

Johnny's total training program incorporated a variety of studio and

Spinning Your Way to Fitness

It was inevitable that Spinning—an indoor cycling workout that's set to music and led by a trained instructor—would catch on. Why? Because it's an effective workout almost anyone can do. If you're a cyclist, Spinning is an innovative training tool that could improve your outdoor riding. For noncyclists, it can provide stress release, weight control, and a beneficial cardiovascular workout.

With Spinning (and similar programs that have cropped up) there's no impact, no age limit, and no competition. Everyone works at their own pace, yet with the energy and benefits of being in a group. At the core of the workout is a stationary bike originally developed by Johnny G for his own Race Across America training and now made by Schwinn. Four main features set it apart from other "exercycles."

☐ The seat and handlebar adjust up and down, as well as fore and aft, to put the rider in a proper cycling position, allowing maximum body efficiency and comfort.

☐ A fixed gear lets the rider stand and pedal, as on a real bike. Because the fixed gear prevents freewheeling (coasting), the nonstop pedaling action enhances the value of the workout.

☐ The bike's design (which incorporates a 38-pound flywheel) allows quick, smooth, lifelike pedaling in every cadence.

☐ A resistance control knob lets the rider simulate outdoor conditions such as climbing and descending.

During a Spinning workout you might hear pulsating drums for mountain climbs, racing guitars for steep downhills, and ocean waves for recovery. Music becomes the terrain. Instructors use heart-rate monitoring and visualization techniques, as well as the music, to motivate and coach riders toward their individual fitness goals. The basic workout is 40 minutes long. Most facilities offer a variety of classes from beginner to advanced.

outdoor activities—cycling, hiking, martial arts, stretching—that re-
volved around a series of heart-rate intervals to increase fitness and endurance. While working out, everyone wore a heart-rate monitor, so
that over time they could see their progress. In Johnny's terms, this
meant "more performance for less heartbeats." Johnny has a dramatic
spiel about heartbeats being like money in the bank: You have only X
amount in a lifetime, and you surely don't want to waste them.

Johnny's resting heart rate, I learned, was 32. A resting heart rate in
the high 40s or low 50s is enviable. Mine was in the high 60s. I was using
up my precious heartbeat account twice as fast as Johnny. I signed on.

Nearly 5 years later, after working out religiously 5 or 6 days a week,
Spinning and weight training, I was in the best shape of my life. I was
over 50 years old and fitter than I'd been at 35.

Still, the smoking demon controlled me. And what a stigma that was,
especially in California. I couldn't smoke in my kids' or friends' houses,
and they didn't even like coming to mine because of "the smell." And
every time I tried to quit, I'd gain 5 or 10 pounds, despite all of my
training.

The Showdown

That summer, Johnny introduced Super Saturdays, a series of 12-hour
endurance workout days that included bike rides, morning and after-
noon mountain hikes, stretching sessions, Spinning, running stadium
steps, and mile runs. Being 10 years older than anyone else in the group,
I was sure that this was out of my league. But Johnny worked on me. I
owed it to myself to try, he insisted, and he would help me and let me go
at my own pace. I agreed to try.

As it turned out, at the end of the day, bone tired, with blisters on all
10 toes, I'd done it, thanks to Johnny's coaxing and cajoling and an endurance I didn't know I had. And there to see me going through that
profound breakthrough experience was a guest participant, Chris
Kostman—like Johnny, a former RAAM solo rider. When he popped the
Team RAAM question I said yes. After all, I'd broken a mental barrier
and now everything was possible—even the Race Across America.

Victory

Armed with the decision to do RAAM and a 3-month supply of nico-
tine patches, I quit smoking on Christmas Day, 1994. Two weeks after
the patches ended, my resting heart rate dropped 10 beats. After 6 more

months of training, it was 52. By Christmas 1995 it was 46. This was the most powerful incentive to never smoke again. I'd been squandering my heartbeat account and was finally rebuilding it.

Meanwhile, as a result of an article I'd written in *Silver Streak*, a newsletter for 50-plus women cyclists, I met Dr. Arnie Baker, San Diego physician, author, and nationally recognized cycling guru. He agreed to be our coach, and the RAAM team came together: Jeanette Marsh from Mississippi, Sharon Koontz from North Carolina, Celeste Callahan from Colorado, and yours truly from Southern California. For the next year and a half we turned our lives over to the organizational challenge of training and event logistics—all done by e-mail. (Just imagine four women debating the design of a jersey using personal computers!)

Arnie created an overall team training program, adjusted for our differences in experience and climate. The program focused on endurance—piles of miles. As Arnie advised, our first goal as RAAM rookies was to finish. From September 1995 our five or six weekly training rides increased 10 miles each week, all the way up to a 600-mile week in mid-February 1996.

From then until June, high-mileage days alternated with speedwork days—interval training done in three or four short rides per day to simulate the shifts we'd be riding in RAAM. In June, as the last leg of my distance training, I did an organized 3-week ride called PAC Tour, which went from Chicago to Santa Monica on Route 66, averaging 110 miles per day at touring pace. Celeste joined us the first week. By July our team was tapering down, counting down, and nerving up.

A Ride for the Record

Everyone said it was the most temperate weather RAAM had experienced in years. The California desert had been only 100 degrees, the top of Wolf Creek Pass in the Colorado Rockies was not below freezing, and the headwinds in Oklahoma weren't devastating. So we couldn't really complain as those Tennessee mountains tapered into an all-day driving rain on excruciatingly deep rollers in Georgia for the last 400 miles. Georgia: the last day, the last state. Six and a half days so far—156 nonstop hours for this team of four riders and 16 hard-working crew members—and they had passed without serious casualty.

Even as we robotically continued our final shifts, the tiniest celebration neurons (that we thought might be dead) began to spark. I started envisioning the finish line. A crowd would be there applauding; this is a magnet that pulls you in. At around 4:00 A.M. on Monday, the ESPN2 video car pulled alongside to film our finish—concrete evidence that there truly was an end.

The official finish this year was in Pooler, just on the outskirts of Savannah. Solo riders or teams had to wait here and serve time penalties if they had broken any rules (we hadn't). It also allowed teams to put all of their riders on the road at once for a parade ride to the finish line in Savannah, where the full elapsed time for RAAM would be recorded.

Monday, August 11, 5:30 A.M. For the first time since our training camp 5 months earlier, our team rode together. The beautiful Savannah riverfront appeared deserted and glowing under streetlights, creating a surreal effect, as though the city had come to a halt to welcome us. In a few minutes I would see my son and grandson holding the ribbon across the finish line, as about a hundred friends, family and RAAM officials cheered us in and congratulated us with a thrilling award ceremony. Exhausted and joyously triumphant, we stood with our crew on the podium to receive gold medals and wonderful hand-carved RAAM plaques. Seven days, 17 hours, and 50 minutes had passed since we left California. No 50-plus women's team had ever before entered RAAM. We did it! We set a world record.

Phyllis Cohen, a writer, is 59 and has been smoke-free for nearly 8 years.

Anatomy of a Bike

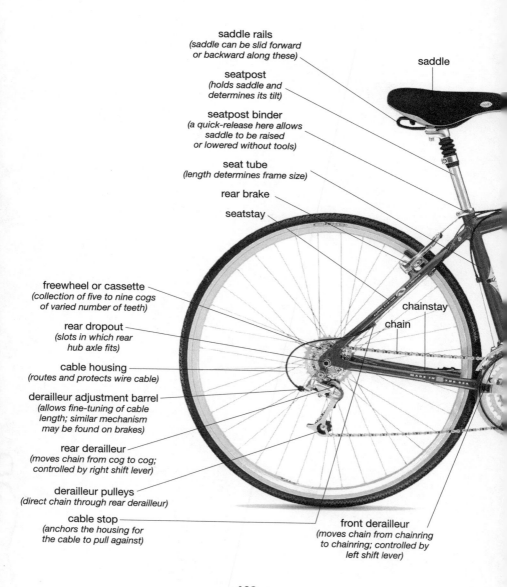

saddle rails
(saddle can be slid forward or backward along these)

saddle

seatpost
(holds saddle and determines its tilt)

seatpost binder
(a quick-release here allows saddle to be raised or lowered without tools)

seat tube
(length determines frame size)

rear brake

seatstay

freewheel or cassette
(collection of five to nine cogs of varied number of teeth)

chainstay

chain

rear dropout
(slots in which rear hub axle fits)

cable housing
(routes and protects wire cable)

derailleur adjustment barrel
(allows fine-tuning of cable length; similar mechanism may be found on brakes)

rear derailleur
(moves chain from cog to cog; controlled by right shift lever)

derailleur pulleys
(direct chain through rear derailleur)

cable stop
(anchors the housing for the cable to pull against)

front derailleur
(moves chain from chainring to chainring; controlled by left shift lever)

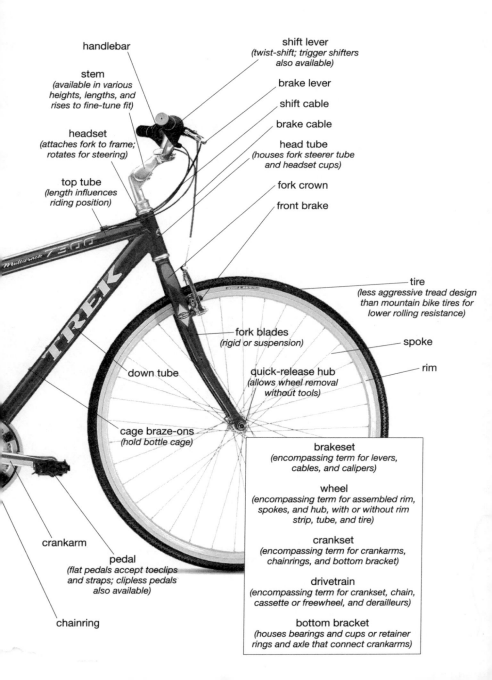

handlebar

stem
*(available in various
heights, lengths, and
rises to fine-tune fit)*

headset
*(attaches fork to frame;
rotates for steering)*

top tube
*(length influences
riding position)*

down tube

cage braze-ons
(hold bottle cage)

crankarm

pedal
*(flat pedals accept toeclips
and straps; clipless pedals
also available)*

chainring

shift lever
*(twist-shift; trigger shifters
also available)*

brake lever

shift cable

brake cable

head tube
*(houses fork steerer tube
and headset cups)*

fork crown

front brake

tire
*(less aggressive tread design
than mountain bike tires for
lower rolling resistance)*

fork blades
(rigid or suspension)

quick-release hub
*(allows wheel removal
without tools)*

spoke

rim

brakeset
*(encompassing term for levers,
cables, and calipers)*

wheel
*(encompassing term for assembled rim,
spokes, and hub, with or without rim
strip, tube, and tire)*

crankset
*(encompassing term for crankarms,
chainrings, and bottom bracket)*

drivetrain
*(encompassing term for crankset, chain,
cassette or freewheel, and derailleurs)*

bottom bracket
*(houses bearings and cups or retainer
rings and axle that connect crankarms)*

Glossary

A

Aerobic: Exercise at an intensity that allows the body's need for oxygen to be continually met. This intensity can be sustained for long periods.

Anaerobic: Exercise above the intensity at which the body's need for oxygen can be met. This intensity can be sustained only briefly.

B

Bar-ends: Short pieces attached to the ends of a flat handlebar to provide an alternate hand position.

Bonk: To run out of energy, usually because the rider has failed to eat or drink enough.

Bottom bracket: The part of the bike frame where the crankset is installed.

BPM: Abbreviation for "beats per minute" in reference to heart rate.

C

Cadence: The number of times during 1 minute that a pedal stroke is completed. Also called pedal rpm.

Century: A ride of 100 miles or 100 kilometers (called a metric century).

Chondromalacia: A softening or wearing away and cracking of the cartilage under the kneecap, resulting in pain and inflammation.

Cleat: A fitting attached to the sole of the shoe for engaging the pedal.

Clipless: Refers to a type of pedal. Cleats bolted to the shoes' soles lock into the pedals to hold feet securely, allowing a more powerful and efficient pedal stroke. Feet are released by pivoting them laterally.

D

Downshift: To shift to a lower gear, that is, to a larger cog or smaller chainring.

Drops: The lower portion of a down-turned drop handlebar, typically found on a road bike.

E

Effective Cycling: A bicycling education program run by the League of American Bicyclists that teaches riding skills and other elements of safe, efficient cycling.

G

Glutes: The gluteal muscles of the buttocks. They are key to pedaling power.

Glycogen: A fuel derived as glucose (sugar) from carbohydrate and stored in the muscles and liver. It's the primary energy source for high-intensity cycling. Reserves are normally depleted after about 2½ hours of riding.

Granny gear: The lowest gear ratio, combining the small chainring with the largest cassette cog. It's mainly used for very steep climbs.

H

Hamstrings: The muscles on the backs of the thighs, which are not well-developed by cycling.

Hooks: The curved portions of a down-turned drop handlebar, typically found on a road bike.

I

Interval training: A type of workout in which periods of intense effort are alternated with periods of easy effort for recovery.

L

Lactic acid: A substance formed during anaerobic metabolism when there is incomplete breakdown of glucose. It rapidly produces muscle fatigue and pain. Also called lactate.

M

Max VO_2: The maximum amount of oxygen that can be consumed during all-out exertion. This is a key indicator of a person's potential in cycling and other aerobic sports. It's largely genetically determined but can be improved somewhat by training.

O

Overtraining: Long-lasting physical and mental fatigue resulting from the stress of too much work without enough rest.

P

Paceline: A group formation (often single file) in which each rider takes a turn breaking the oncoming wind at the front before pulling over, dropping to the rear position, and riding in the others' draft until reaching the front again.

Pedal rpm: *See* Cadence.

Pushing: Pedaling with a relatively slow cadence, using larger gears.

Q

Quadriceps: The muscle group on the fronts of the thighs, which are well-developed by cycling.

R

Rails: On a saddle, the metal undercarriage that is clamped by the seatpost. Rails can be steel or lighter materials such as titanium or manganese.

Repetition: Also called rep. In weight or interval training, each individual exertion. For example, if you press a barbell five times or do a series of five sprints, you are doing five reps.

Resistance trainer: A stationary training device into which the bike is clamped. Pedaling resistance increases with pedaling speed to simulate actual riding. Also known as an indoor, wind, or mag trainer. (The last two names are derived from the fan or magnet that creates resistance on the rear wheel.)

S

Saddle sores: Skin problems in the crotch that develop from chafing caused by pedaling action. Sores can range from minor raw spots to boil-like lesions if infection occurs.

Set: In weight or interval training, one group of repetitions. For example, if you do eight reps three times you are doing three sets.

Spinning: Pedaling with a relatively fast cadence using low to moderate gears.

Standover height: The distance from the ground to the top of a bike's top tube. Depending on bike type, it should be at least 2 inches less than the rider's inseam length to allow for safe dismounts.

T

Time trial: A solo race against the clock. Each rider leaves the start at a certain interval (usually 1 minute) and the winner is the one who completes the course in the shortest time.

Toeclips: Metal or plastic cages that are attached to conventional pedals to keep feet in the proper position. Usually used with toe straps that allow the feet to be tightened to the pedals.

U

Upshift: To shift to a higher gear, that is, to a smaller cog or larger chainring.

Index

Boldface page references indicate photographs or illustrations.
Underscored page references indicate boxed text.

A

Abdominal crunch exercise, 72–73
ACOG, 65–66
Adjusting bike, 57–58, 60, **60**
Alertness, safety and, 8
American College of Obstetrics and
    Gynecology (ACOG), 65–66
Anatomic saddle, 30
Anatomy of bike, **108**–9
Anticipation, safety and, 11–12
Apparel. *See* Clothes
At-home workout, 72–73
Avocet, 30, 33

B

Back hyperextension exercise, 73
Beaters, 7
Biceps curl exercise, 73
Bicycling Federation of America, 9
Bicycling magazine
    editors of, 21–26, 41–48
    Fitness Advisory Board, 85–90
Bicycling Magazine's Basic
    Maintenance and Repair, 49
Bike. *See also specific components and*
    types
    adjusting, 57–58, 60, **60**
    anatomy of, **108**–9
    carrying capacity of, 22
    cleaning, 56
    components of, 25–26
    cost of, 23–24
    crashing, 14–16, 66
    inspecting, 57
    lubing, 56–57, **57**
    selecting, 22–23
    size of, 25
    storing, 55–56
    technology, 23
    theft, preventing, 7, 14
    tightening, 57
    tips for caring for, 55–57, 55, **56**, **57**,
        60, **60**
    types of, 21–22
    women's, 26–30
Bike trailer, 89
Birth control pills, 64–65
Bonking, 79
Brake levers
    mountain bike, 26
    road bike, 26, 41–42
    selecting, 26
    women's bike, 29
Burns, Kathy, 98–100
Butt
    cycling and, 74–77
    mountain bike and, 46
    riding position and, 75–76
    road bike and, 42–43

C

Calorie
    consumption, 82–83
    requirement, 78–79

Carbohydrates, 67, 77–79

Carpenter, Connie, 3, 93–98

Carpenter/Phinney Women's Bike
        Camp, 3, 93–98

Carrying capacity of bike, 22

Cell phone, safety and, 8

Century ride, 90

Classes, cycling, 9, 93–98

Cleaning bike, 56

Clothes. *See also specific types*
    color of, 11
    loose, 7
    safety and, 7, 11
    selecting, 35–38

Clubs, cycling, 87. *See also specific
        organizations*

Cohen, Phyllis, 101–6

Color of clothes, safety and, 11

Comfort bike, 21

Components of bike, 25–26. *See also
        specific types*

Confidence, cycling with, 6–9

Cost of bike, 23–24

Cover-ups, 37

Crankarms
    mountain bike, 48
    road bike, 44
    women's bike, 28

Crashing, 14–16, 66

Crop tops, 37

Cross bike, 21

Cruiser, 21

Cuerdon, Carlotta, 48–50, <u>68–69</u>

Cycling, 3, 4. *See also* Opportunities
        for cycling
    butt and, 74–77
    with children in tow, 89
    with confidence, 6–9
    endurance days of, 86

    goals, 86–87
    in groups, 22
    improvement in, 85–86
    with men, 4–6
    moderate days of, 86
    overweight and, 86
    questions and answers, 85–90
    speed days of, 86–87
    terms, 111–13

Cycling classes and schools, 9, 93–98

Cycling clubs, 87. *See also specific
        organizations*

D

DeMoss, Virginia, 77–85

Diet
    calories and, 78–79, <u>82–83</u>
    carbohydrates and, 67, 73–79
    energy drinks and, 79–80
    fats and, 80–81
    menstrual cycle and, 64
    pregnancy and, 66–67
    proteins and, 82–84
    supplements and, 84–85
    weight loss and, 81–82

Dietary fats, 80–81

Drinking, 79–80

Dual density saddle, 34, **34**

Dual suspension, 24

Durometers, <u>58</u>

E

Effective Cycling class, 9

Elastomer fork, <u>58–59</u>

Endurance days of cycling, 86

Energy drinks, 79–80

Equipment, 19. *See also* Bike; Clothes

Estrogen, 63, 65

Exercises, strengthening, 72–73

F

Falling, 14–16, 66
Fats, dietary, 80–81
Fear of falling, 14–16
Fitness, 4–6, 22
Flat tire, fixing, 50–54, **50–54**, <u>53</u>, <u>54</u>
Fragnoli, Delaine, <u>58–59</u>, 70–77
Frame
 mountain bike, 47
 road bike, 43
 women's bike, 27
Front suspension, 24, <u>58–59</u>
Fruit juice, 80

G

Garvey, Ellen, 19–20
Gloves, 37
Glycogen, 79
Goals, cycling, 86–87
Group cycling, 22

H

Handlebar
 mountain bike, 45
 road bike, 41
 selecting, 26
 women's bike, 28
Harassment, handling, <u>12–13</u>
Heart-rate monitor (HRM), 87–88
Helmets, 13–14, 38
Henry, Sara J., 6–9, 26–30, 65–69
HRM, 87–88
Hybrid bike, 21, 23
Hydration, 79–80

I

Improvement in cycling, 85–86
Inflating tire, 53–54, **53**, 56, **56**
Inspecting bike, 57

Instincts, listening to, 8
Ischial tuberosities, 30–31, 42, 74–75

J

Jackets, 37
Jerseys, 37

K

Knee pain, 90
Knickers, 36
Knowledge, power and, 7

L

Langley, Jim, 50–57, 60
Lateral shoulder raise exercise, 73
League of American Bicyclists, 9
Locking system, helmet, 38
Lubing bike, 56–57, **57**

M

Maintenance. *See* Repairs and
  maintenance
Mechanics. *See* Pedaling technique;
  Repairs and maintenance;
  Riding position
Melpomene Institute, 66–67
Menstrual cycle, 63–65
Mineral supplements, 67, 84–85
Moderate days of cycling, 86
Moss, Debra Baukney, 4–6
Mountain bike, 21
 brake levers, 26
 butt and, 46
 competition, 98–100, <u>100</u>
 cost of, 24
 crankarms, 48
 frame, 47
 handlebar, 45
 riding position, 44–48, **46**

Mountain bike *(continued)*
  saddle, 32–33, 46–47
  seatpost, 47
  stem, 45
Muscle, strengthening
  at-home workout for, 72–73
  century ride and, 90
  cycling goals for, 86–87
  differences between genders, 70–71
  exercises for, 72–73
  power and, 70–73
  recovery and, 87
  size of muscle and, 90
  weight training and, 71–72

N

National Off-Road Bicycle Association
  (NORBA), <u>100</u>
Nationals (Mount Snow, Vermont), 99
NORBA, <u>100</u>

O

Opportunities for cycling
  mountain bike competitions,
    98–100, <u>100</u>
  Race Across America, 101–6
  road bike school, 93–98
  Spinning classes, 102–4, <u>103</u>
Oral contraceptives, 64–65
Organized rides, 87
Overheating, 66
Overtraining, 88
Overweight, cycling and, 86

P

Pedaling technique, 44, 47–48
Period, menstrual, 63–65
Perspiration, 89

Physical condition. *See also* Diet;
  Fitness
  of butt, 74–77
  heart-rate monitor and, 87–88
  knee pain and, 90
  menstrual cycle and, 63–65
  of muscle, 70–73
  overtraining and, 88
  perspiration and, 89
  pregnancy and, 65–69, <u>68–69</u>
  training sessions and, 88
Pill, the, 64–65
Pisaneschi, Penny, 93–98
Position on bike. *See* Riding position
Power, muscle strengthening and,
  70–73
Predictable cycling behavior, safety
  and, 10
Pregnancy, 65–69, <u>68–69</u>
Preload, <u>59</u>
Progesterone, 63
Proteins, 82–84

Q

QR hubs, 51, **51**, 54, **54**
Questions and answers, cycling, 85–90
Quick-release (QR) hubs, 51, **51**, 54,
  54

R

Race Across America (RAAM), 85,
  101–6
Racing bike, 21–22
RAD, 43–44
RDA, 83
Reach, comfort and, 25
Recommended Dietary Allowance
  (RDA), 83

Recovery, 87

Reflective bands, 11

Repairs and maintenance

  books on, 7, 49

  confidence and, 6–7

  do-it-yourself, 48–50

  flat tire, 50–54, **50–54**, <u>53</u>, <u>54</u>

  front suspension, <u>58–59</u>

  practicing, 7

  tips, 55–57, 60

Riding position

  butt and, 75–76

  mountain bike, 44–48, **46**

  pregnancy and, 67

  road bike, 41–44, **42**

  saddle and, 20

  scorching and, 20

Road bike, 21

  brake levers, 26, 41–42

  butt and, 42–43

  crankarms, 44

  frame, 43

  handlebar, 41

  riding position, 41–44, **42**

  saddles, 33–35, 43

  school, 93–98

  stem, 41

Road rage, avoiding, 7, 12

Rotational Adjustment Device (RAD),
  43–44

Route

  announcing, 7

  selecting, 10–11

S

Saddle

  anatomic, 30

  contact with, 19–20, 30–32

  gender and, 19–20, 25

  height, 43

  mountain bike, 32–33, 46–47

  riding position and, 20

  road bike, 33–35, 43

  selecting, 25

  shock-absorbing seatpost with, <u>31</u>

  tilt, 43

  types of, 32–35

  women's bike, 28–29

Safety

  alertness and, 8

  anticipation and, 11–12

  cell phone and, 8

  clothes and, 7, 11

  helmet and, 13–14

  predictability and, 10

  reflective bands and, 11

  road rage and, avoiding, 12

  route, 7, 10–11

  signaling turns and, 10

  socializing and, 13

  stereo earphones and, avoiding, 87

  traffic and, riding with, 9–10

Schools, cycling, 9, 93–98

Scorching, 20

Seat. *See* Saddle

Seated row exercise, 73

Seatpost, <u>31</u>, 47

Selecting bike, 22–23, 29

Shirts, 37

Shock-absorbing seatpost, <u>31</u>

Shoes, 38

Shorts, 36

Signaling turns, 10

Sit bones, 30–31, 42, 74–75

Size of bike, 25

Socializing, safety and, 13

Soft-ride kits, 58–59

Sorenson, Susan, 9–14

Speed days of cycling, 86–87

Spinning classes, 102–4, 103

Sport touring bike, 21

Stem
    mountain bike, 45
    road bike, 41
    selecting, 26
    women's bike, 27–28

Stereo earphones, avoiding, 87

Storing bike, 55–56

Street savvy. *See* Safety

Strength discrepancy, gender, 70–71

Stuart, Robin, 14–16, 59

Supplements, vitamin and mineral,
    67, 84–85

Suspension forks, 58–59

T

Tandem bike, 23

Technology, bike, 23

Terry Precision Cycling for Women,
    34

Theft, preventing bike, 7, 14

Tightening bike, 57

Tights, 36

Time trialing, 97

Tire
    fixing flat, 50–54, **50–54**, 53, 54
    inflating, 53–54, **53**, 56, **56**
    removing and installing tube on,
        51–52, **52**

Tools and supplies
    bike care, 55
    tire repair, 55

Tops, 37

Touring bike, sport, 21

Traffic, riding with, 9–10

Training, 79, 87–88

Training log, 64

Triceps extension exercise, 73

Trouble while cycling, dealing with,
    7–9

Tube, removing and installing, 51–52,
    52

U

Unisex saddle, 34–35, **35**

Upright row exercise, 73

V

Vitamin supplements, 67, 84–85

W

Walsh, Julie, 63–65

Weaver, Susan, 12–13, 35–38

Weight loss, 81–82, 86, 90

Weight training, 71–72

Wheel, removing and installing, 51,
    51, 54, **54**

WOMBATS (Women's Mountain Bike
    and Tea Society), 9

Women's bike, 26–30

Women's cycling school, 93–98

Workout, at-home, 72–73

About the Authors

Kathy Burns, a mountain biker, achieved her goal of qualifying for the World Masters Team and competed at the Worlds in Quebec in September 1998.

Connie Carpenter won the first-ever Olympic road race for women in 1984. She and her husband, ex-pro Davis Phinney, who also competed in the 1984 Olympics, operate the Carpenter/Phinney Cycling Camps in Boulder, Colorado.

Phyllis Cohen, 59 and smoke-free for nearly 8 years, is a cyclist and writer in Los Angeles. She's working on a book called *Age Is an Attitude: The Secrets and Tips of Fit Women over Fifty*.

Carlotta Cuerdon is an associate editor with *Bicycling* magazine.

Virginia DeMoss specializes in writing about sports nutrition.

Delaine Fragnoli is a *Bicycling* magazine contributing editor.

Ellen Garvey is a college English professor in New Jersey.

Sara J. Henry is a Tennessee-based freelance writer.

Jim Langley is a former *Bicycling* magazine technical editor and author of *Bicycling Magazine's Complete Guide to Bicycle Maintenance and Repair*.

Debra Baukney Moss is a freelance writer as well as an improving cyclist.

Penny Pisaneschi races on the roads and trails in northern California, where she works in sales for a software company.

Susan Sorensen is a former editor at *Bicycling* magazine.

Robin Stuart is the author of *Mountain Biking for Women* and a mountain biking instructor.

Julie Walsh is a triathlete, registered dietitian, and New York City–based freelance writer who specializes in women's health issues.

Susan Weaver is a Pennsylvania-based freelance writer and former editor at *Bicycling* magazine. She is the author of *A Woman's Guide to Cycling*.